This planner belongs to :

____

Twenty-four

January

S	M	T	W	T	F	S
	1	2	3	4	5	6
7	8	9	10	11	12	13
14	15	16	17	18	19	20
21	22	23	24	25	26	27
28	29	30	31			

February

S	M	T	W	T	F	S
				1	2	3
4	5	6	7	8	9	10
11	12	13	14	15	16	17
18	19	20	21	22	23	24
25	26	27	28	29		

March

S	M	T	W	T	F	S
					1	2
3	4	5	6	7	8	9
10	11	12	13	14	15	16
17	18	19	20	21	22	23
24	25	26	27	28	29	30
31						

April

S	M	T	W	T	F	S
	1	2	3	4	5	6
7	8	9	10	11	12	13
14	15	16	17	18	19	20
21	22	23	24	25	26	27
28	29	30				

May

S	M	T	W	T	F	S
			1	2	3	4
5	6	7	8	9	10	11
12	13	14	15	16	17	18
19	20	21	22	23	24	25
26	27	28	29	30	31	

June

S	M	T	W	T	F	S
						1
2	3	4	5	6	7	8
9	10	11	12	13	14	15
16	17	18	19	20	21	22
23	24	25	26	27	28	29
30						

July

S	M	T	W	T	F	S
	1	2	3	4	5	6
7	8	9	10	11	12	13
14	15	16	17	18	19	20
21	22	23	24	25	26	27
28	29	30	31			

August

S	M	T	W	T	F	S
				1	2	3
4	5	6	7	8	9	10
11	12	13	14	15	16	17
18	19	20	21	22	23	24
25	26	27	28	29	30	31

September

S	M	T	W	T	F	S
1	2	3	4	5	6	7
8	9	10	11	12	13	14
15	16	17	18	19	20	21
22	23	24	25	26	27	28
29	30					

October

S	M	T	W	T	F	S
		1	2	3	4	5
6	7	8	9	10	11	12
13	14	15	16	17	18	19
20	21	22	23	24	25	26
27	28	29	30	31		

November

S	M	T	W	T	F	S
					1	2
3	4	5	6	7	8	9
10	11	12	13	14	15	16
17	18	19	20	21	22	23
24	25	26	27	28	29	30

December

S	M	T	W	T	F	S
1	2	3	4	5	6	7
8	9	10	11	12	13	14
15	16	17	18	19	20	21
22	23	24	25	26	27	28
29	30	31				

Year in Pixels

	J	F	M	A	M	J	J	A	S	O	N	D
1.												
2.												
3.												
4.												
5.												
6.												
7.												
8.												
9.												
10.												
11.												
12.												
13.												
14.												
15.												
16.												
17.												
18.												
19.												
20.												
21.												
22.												
23.												
24.												
25.												
26.												
27.												
28.												
29.												
30.												
31.												

Color Codes

Notes

January 2024

MONDAY	TUESDAY	WEDNESDAY	THURSDAY
1	2	3	4
8	9	10	11
15	16	17	18
22	23	24	25
29	30	31	

January

FRIDAY	SATURDAY	SUNDAY	NOTES
5	6	7	○
			○
			○
			○
			○
12	13	14	○
			○
			○
			○
19	20	21	○
			○
			○
			○
			○
26	27	28	○
			○
			○
			○
			○
			NOTES

February 2024

MONDAY	TUESDAY	WEDNESDAY	THURSDAY
			1
5	6	7	8
12	13	14	15
19	20	21	22
26	27	28	29

February 2024

FRIDAY	SATURDAY	SUNDAY	NOTES
2	3	4	○
			○
			○
			○
			○
9	10	11	○
			○
			○
			○
16	17	18	○
			○
			○
			○
			○
23	24	25	○
			○
			○
			○
			○
			NOTES

March 2024

MONDAY	TUESDAY	WEDNESDAY	THURSDAY
4	5	6	7
11	12	13	14
18	19	20	21
25	26	27	28

March

FRIDAY	SATURDAY	SUNDAY	NOTES
1	2	3	
8	9	10	
15	16	17	
22	23	24	
29	30	31	NOTES

April 2024

MONDAY	TUESDAY	WEDNESDAY	THURSDAY
1	2	3	4
8	9	10	11
15	16	17	18
22	23	24	25
29	30		

April 2024

FRIDAY	SATURDAY	SUNDAY	NOTES
5	6	7	○
			○
			○
			○
			○
12	13	14	○
			○
			○
			○
19	20	21	○
			○
			○
			○
			○
26	27	28	○
			○
			○
			○
			○
			NOTES

May 2024

MONDAY	TUESDAY	WEDNESDAY	THURSDAY
		1	2
6	7	8	9
13	14	15	16
20	21	22	23
27	28	29	30

May 2024

FRIDAY	SATURDAY	SUNDAY	NOTES
3	4	5	○
			○
			○
			○
			○
10	11	12	○
			○
			○
			○
17	18	19	○
			○
			○
			○
			○
24	25	26	○
			○
			○
			○
			○
31			NOTES

June 2024

MONDAY	TUESDAY	WEDNESDAY	THURSDAY
3	4	5	6
10	11	12	13
17	18	19	20
24	25	26	27

June 2024

FRIDAY	SATURDAY	SUNDAY	NOTES
	1	2	○
			○
			○
			○
			○
7	8	9	○
			○
			○
			○
14	15	16	○
			○
			○
			○
			○
21	22	23	○
			○
			○
			○
			○
28	29	30	NOTES

July 2024

MONDAY	TUESDAY	WEDNESDAY	THURSDAY
1	2	3	4
8	9	10	11
15	16	17	18
22	23	24	25
29	30	31	

FRIDAY	SATURDAY	SUNDAY	NOTES
5	6	7	○
			○
			○
			○
			○
12	13	14	○
			○
			○
			○
19	20	21	○
			○
			○
			○
			○
26	27	28	○
			○
			○
			○
			○
			NOTES

August 2024

MONDAY	TUESDAY	WEDNESDAY	THURSDAY
			1
5	6	7	8
12	13	14	15
19	20	21	22
26	27	28	29

August 2024

FRIDAY	SATURDAY	SUNDAY	NOTES
2	3	4	○
			○
			○
			○
			○
9	10	11	○
			○
			○
			○
16	17	18	○
			○
			○
			○
			○
23	24	25	○
			○
			○
			○
			○
30	31		NOTES

September 2024

MONDAY	TUESDAY	WEDNESDAY	THURSDAY
2	3	4	5
9	10	11	12
16	17	18	19
23	24	25	26

September 2024

FRIDAY	SATURDAY	SUNDAY	NOTES
		1	○
			○
			○
			○
			○
6	7	8	○
			○
			○
			○
13	14	15	○
			○
			○
			○
			○
20	21	22	○
			○
			○
			○
			○
27	28	29	30

October 2024

MONDAY	TUESDAY	WEDNESDAY	THURSDAY
	1	2	3
7	8	9	10
14	15	16	17
21	22	23	24
28	29	30	31

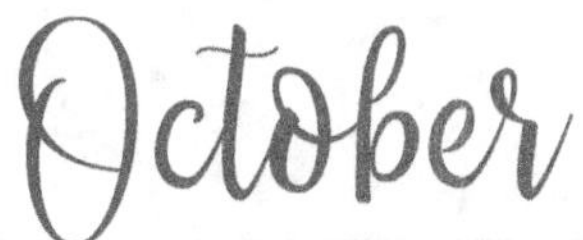

October 2024

FRIDAY	SATURDAY	SUNDAY	NOTES
4	5	6	○
			○
			○
			○
			○
11	12	13	○
			○
			○
			○
18	19	20	○
			○
			○
			○
			○
25	26	27	○
			○
			○
			○
			○
			NOTES

November 2024

MONDAY	TUESDAY	WEDNESDAY	THURSDAY
4	5	6	7
11	12	13	14
18	19	20	21
25	26	27	28

November 2024

FRIDAY	SATURDAY	SUNDAY	NOTES
1	2	3	○
			○
			○
			○
			○
8	9	10	○
			○
			○
			○
15	16	17	○
			○
			○
			○
22	23	24	○
			○
			○
			○
			○
29	30		NOTES

December 2024

MONDAY	TUESDAY	WEDNESDAY	THURSDAY
2	3	4	5
9	10	11	12
16	17	18	19
23	24	25	26

December 2024

FRIDAY	SATURDAY	SUNDAY	NOTES
		1	○
			○
			○
			○
			○
6	7	8	○
			○
			○
			○
13	14	15	○
			○
			○
			○
			○
20	21	22	○
			○
			○
			○
			○
27	28	29	30 / 31

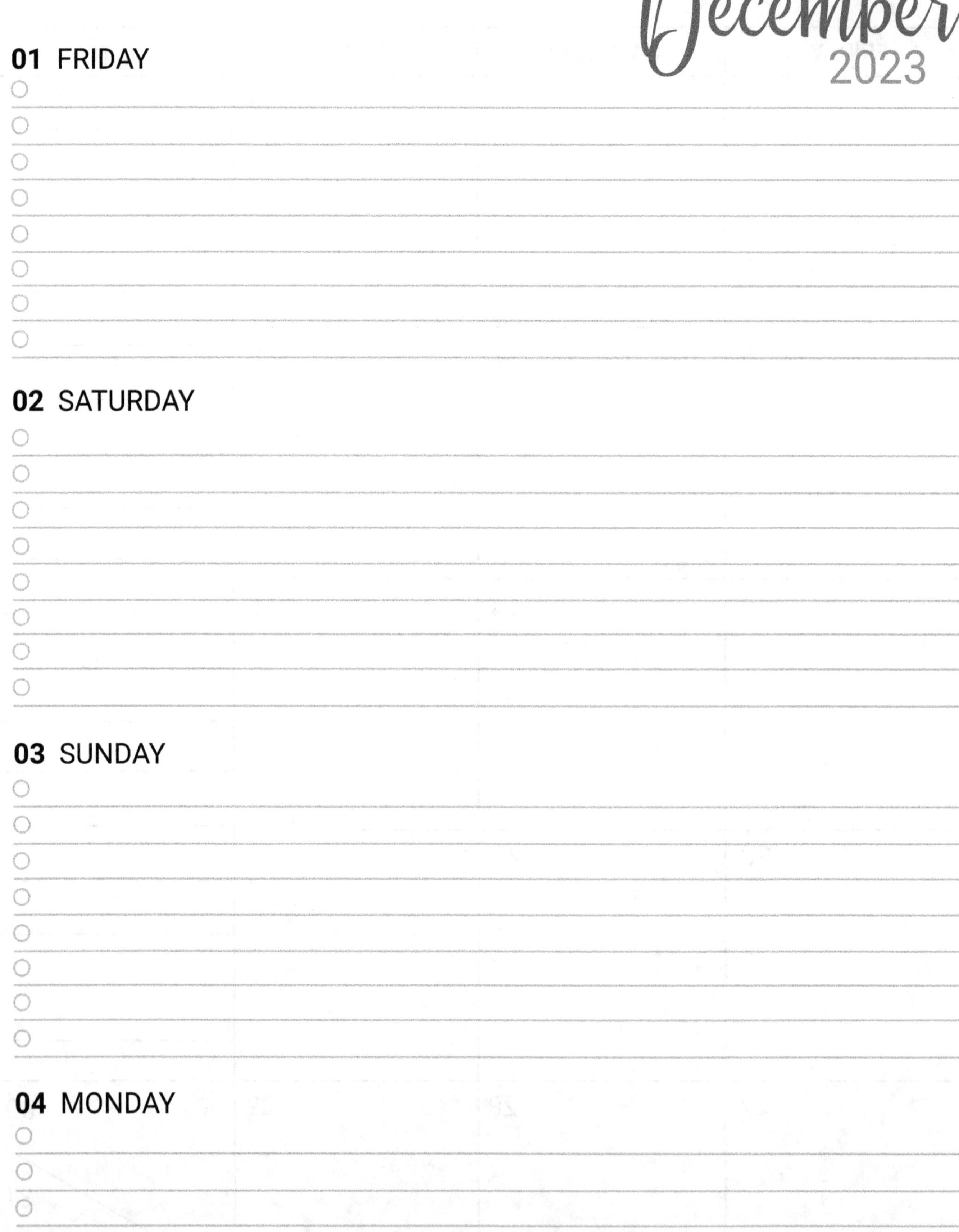

01 FRIDAY

02 SATURDAY

03 SUNDAY

04 MONDAY

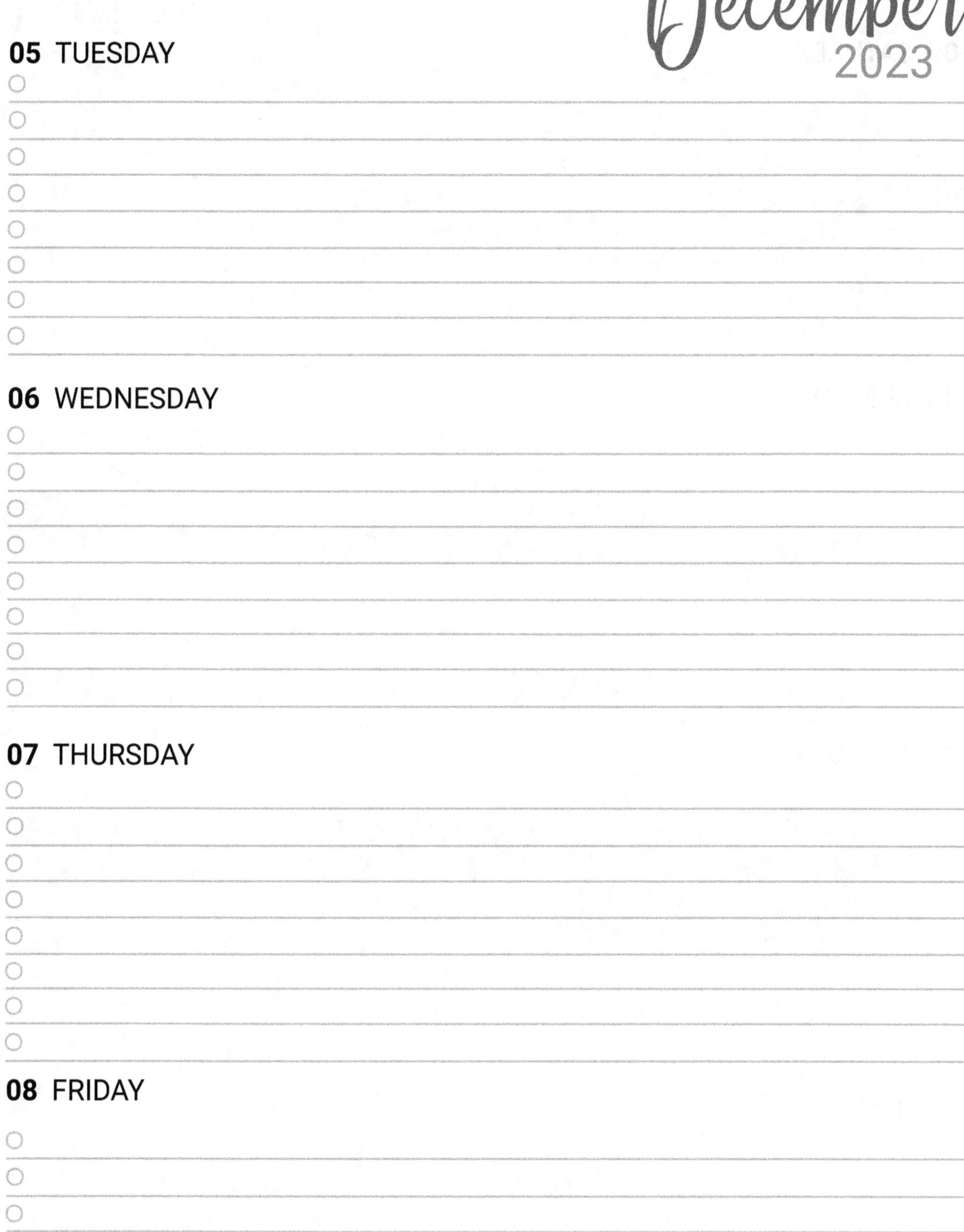

05 TUESDAY

06 WEDNESDAY

07 THURSDAY

08 FRIDAY

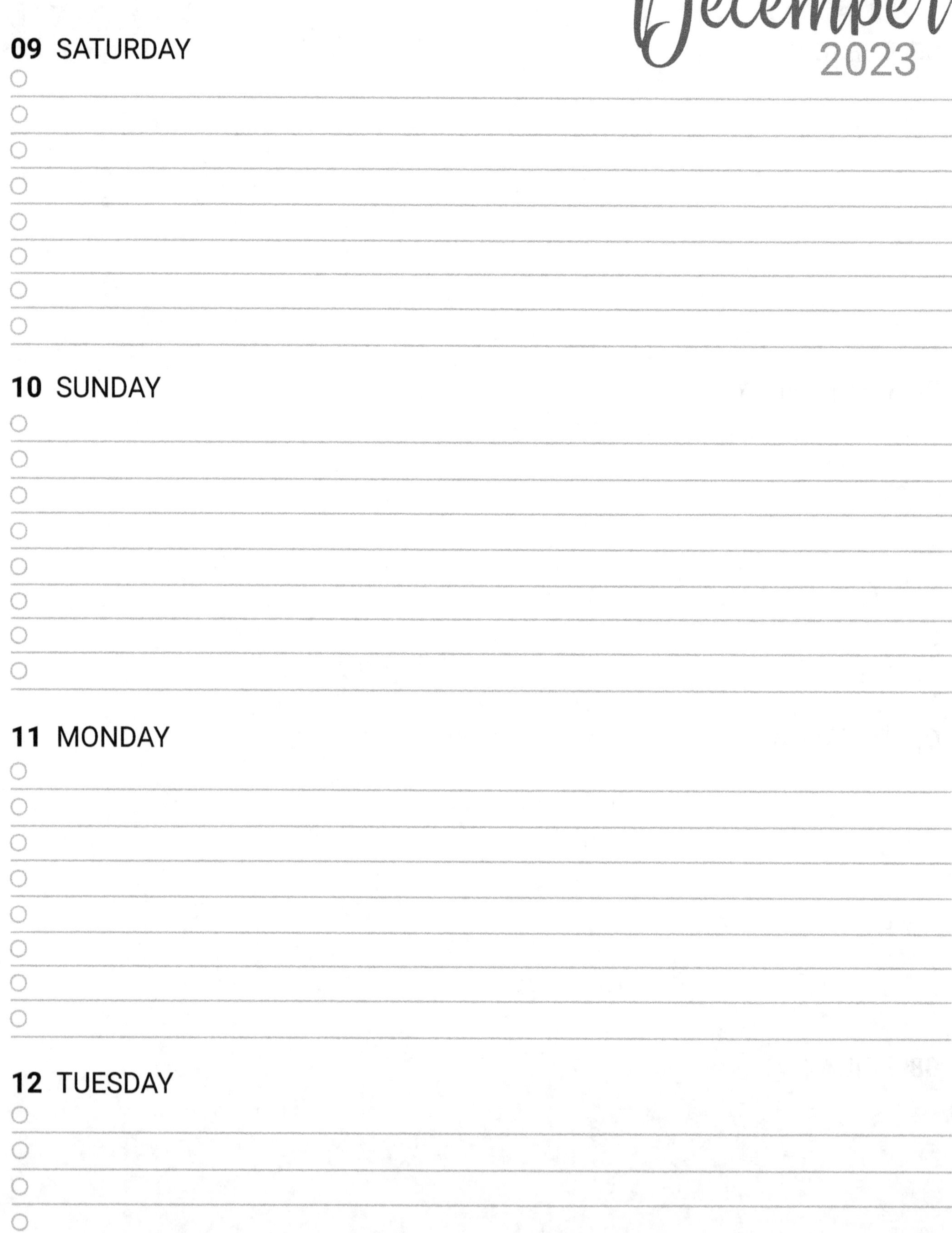

09 SATURDAY

10 SUNDAY

11 MONDAY

12 TUESDAY

December
2023

13 WEDNESDAY

14 THURSDAY

15 FRIDAY

16 SATURDAY

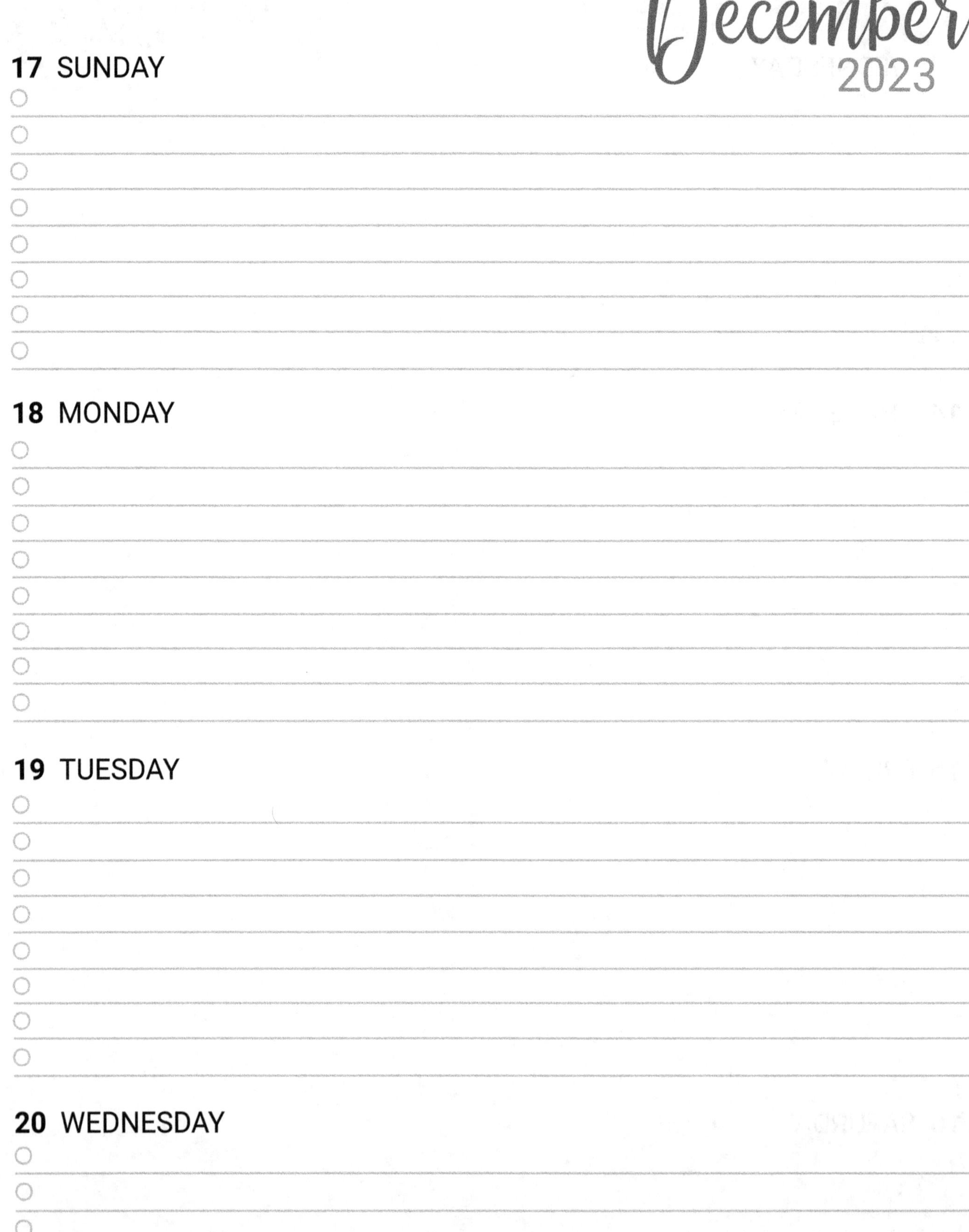

17 SUNDAY

18 MONDAY

19 TUESDAY

20 WEDNESDAY

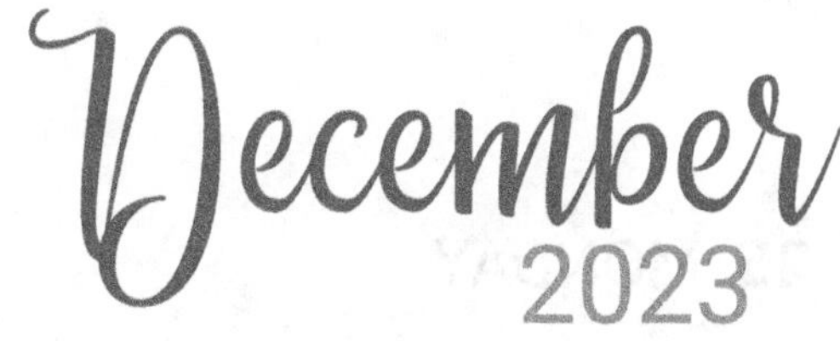

December
2023

21 THURSDAY

22 FRIDAY

23 SATURDAY

24 SUNDAY

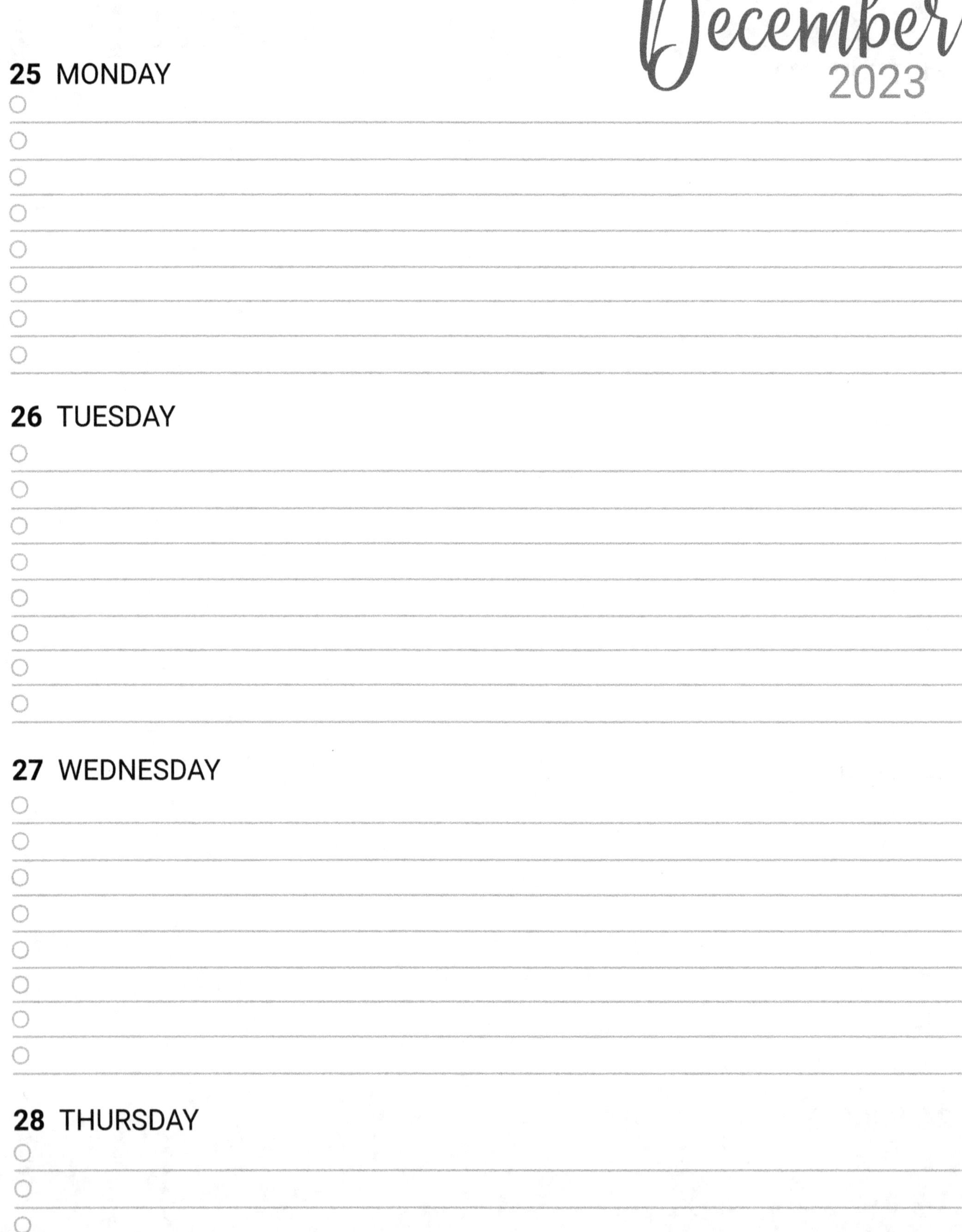

25 MONDAY

26 TUESDAY

27 WEDNESDAY

28 THURSDAY

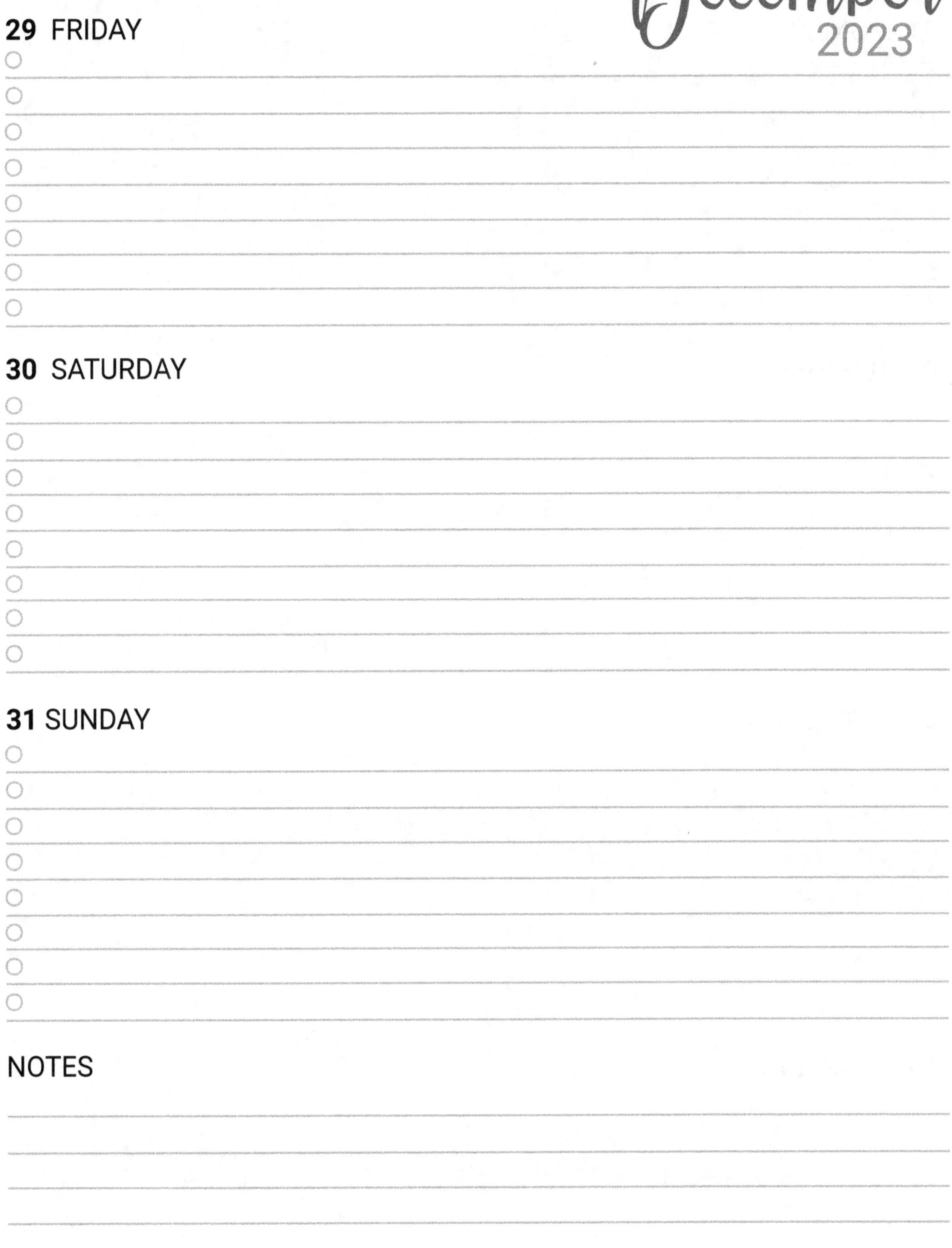

29 FRIDAY

30 SATURDAY

31 SUNDAY

NOTES

01 MONDAY

02 TUESDAY

03 WEDNESDAY

04 THURSDAY

05 FRIDAY

06 SATURDAY

07 SUNDAY

08 MONDAY

09 TUESDAY

10 WEDNESDAY

11 THURSDAY

12 FRIDAY

13 SATURDAY

14 SUNDAY

15 MONDAY

16 TUESDAY

17 WEDNESDAY

18 THURSDAY

19 FRIDAY

20 SATURDAY

January
2024

21 SUNDAY

22 MONDAY

23 TUESDAY

24 WEDNESDAY

January
2024

25 THURSDAY

26 FRIDAY

27 SATURDAY

28 SUNDAY

29 MONDAY

○
○
○
○
○
○
○
○

30 TUESDAY

○
○
○
○
○
○
○
○

31 WEDNESDAY

○
○
○
○
○
○
○
○

NOTES

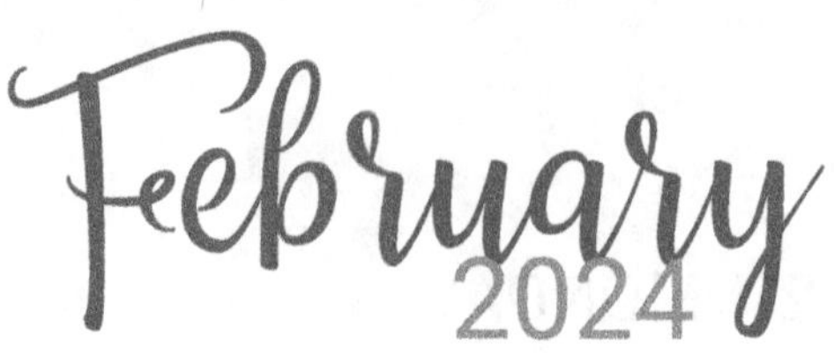

01 THURSDAY

02 FRIDAY

03 SATURDAY

04 SUNDAY

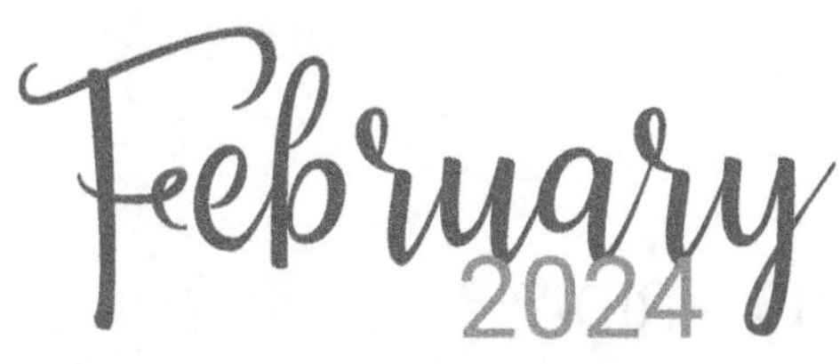

05 MONDAY

06 TUESDAY

07 WEDNESDAY

08 THURSDAY

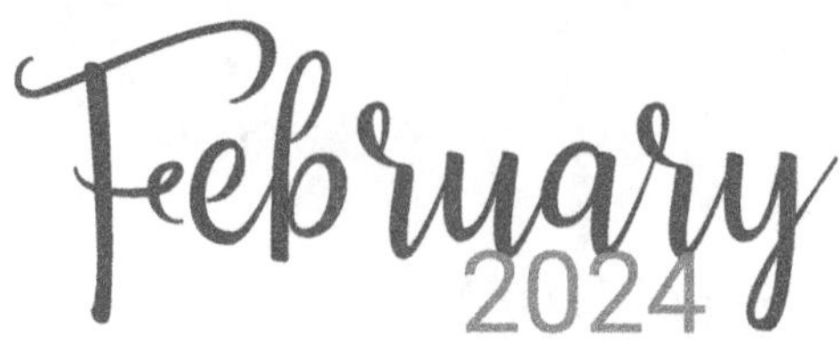

09 FRIDAY

10 SATURDAY

11 SUNDAY

12 MONDAY

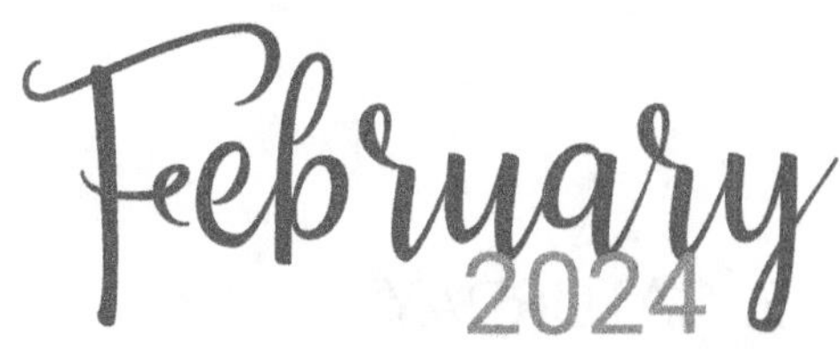

13 TUESDAY

14 WEDNESDAY

15 THURSDAY

16 FRIDAY

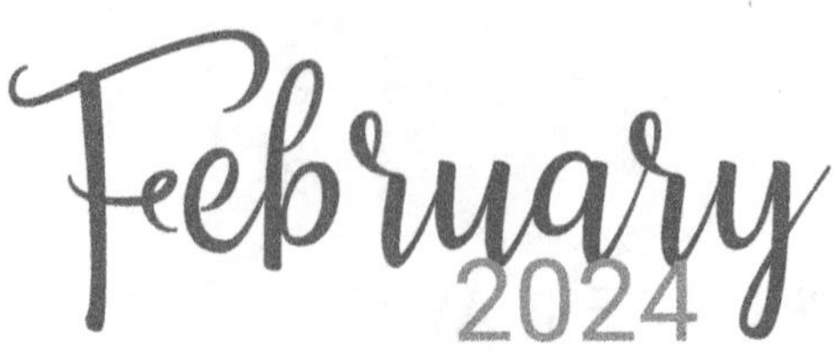

17 SATURDAY

18 SUNDAY

19 MONDAY

20 TUESDAY

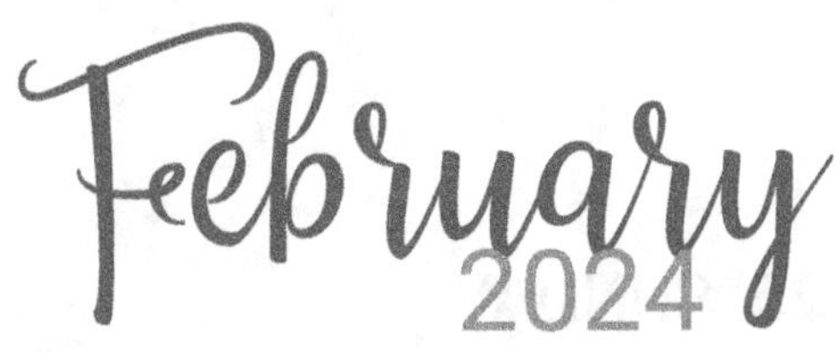

21 WEDNESDAY

22 THURSDAY

23 FRIDAY

24 SATURDAY

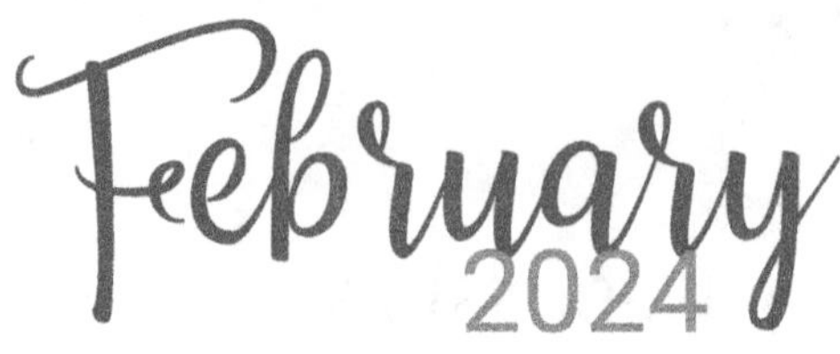

February
2024

25 SUNDAY

26 MONDAY

27 TUESDAY

28 WEDNESDAY

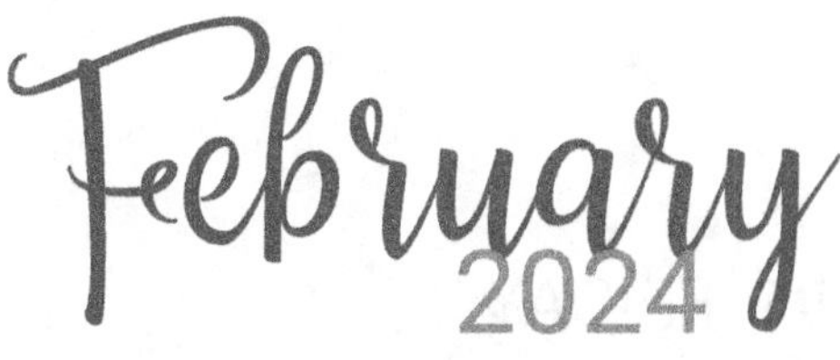

29 THURSDAY

NOTES

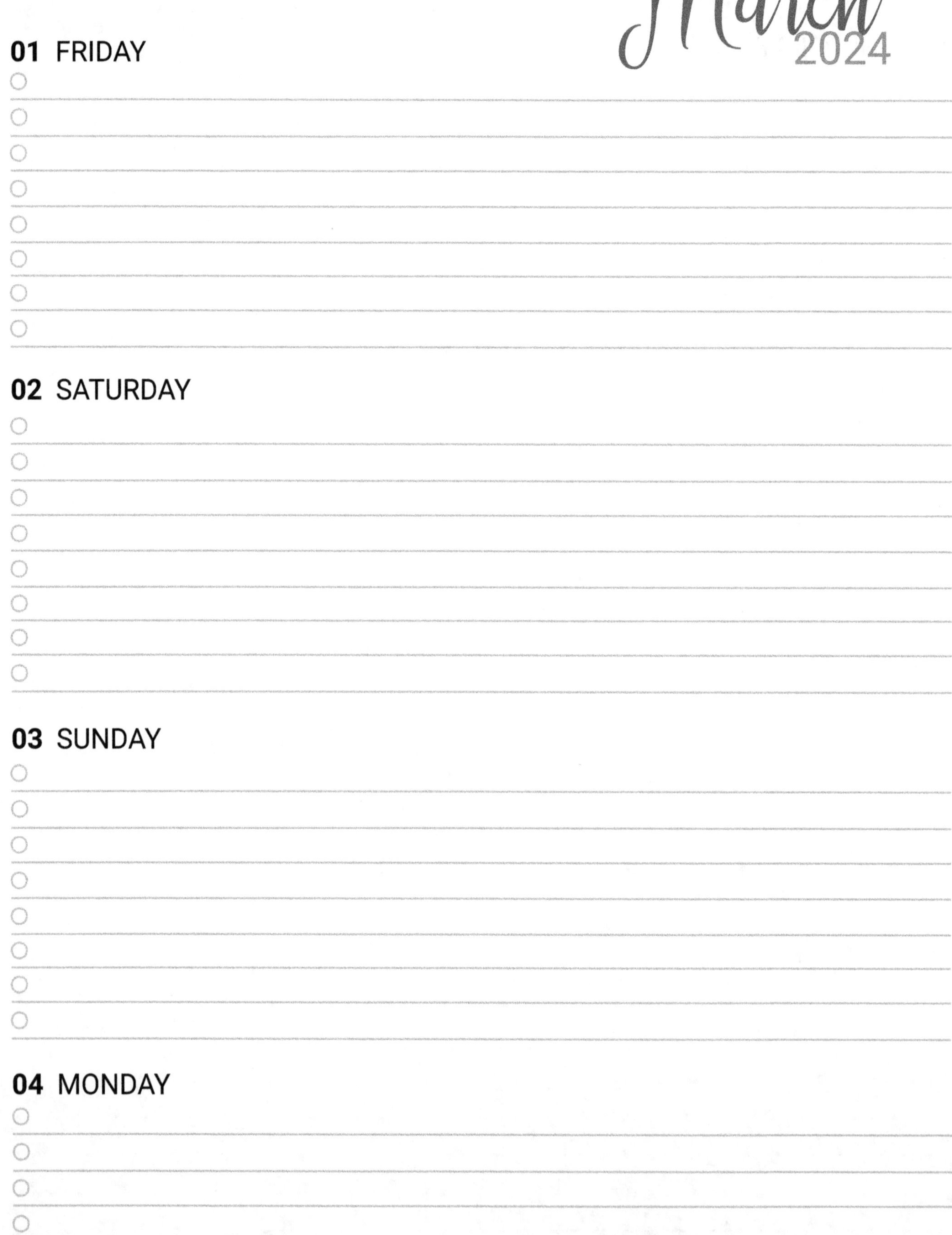

March
2024

01 FRIDAY

02 SATURDAY

03 SUNDAY

04 MONDAY

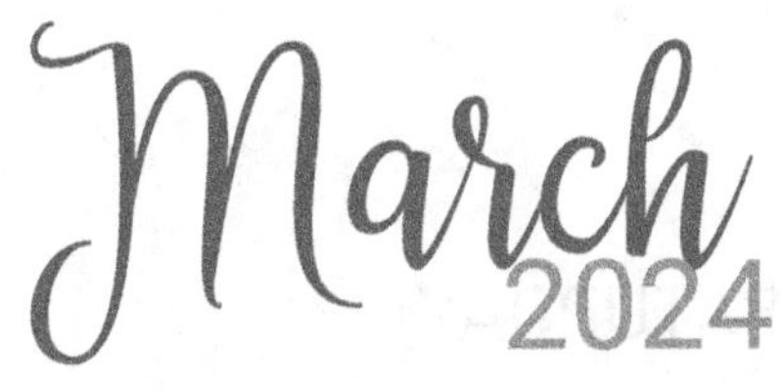

05 TUESDAY

06 WEDNESDAY

07 THURSDAY

08 FRIDAY

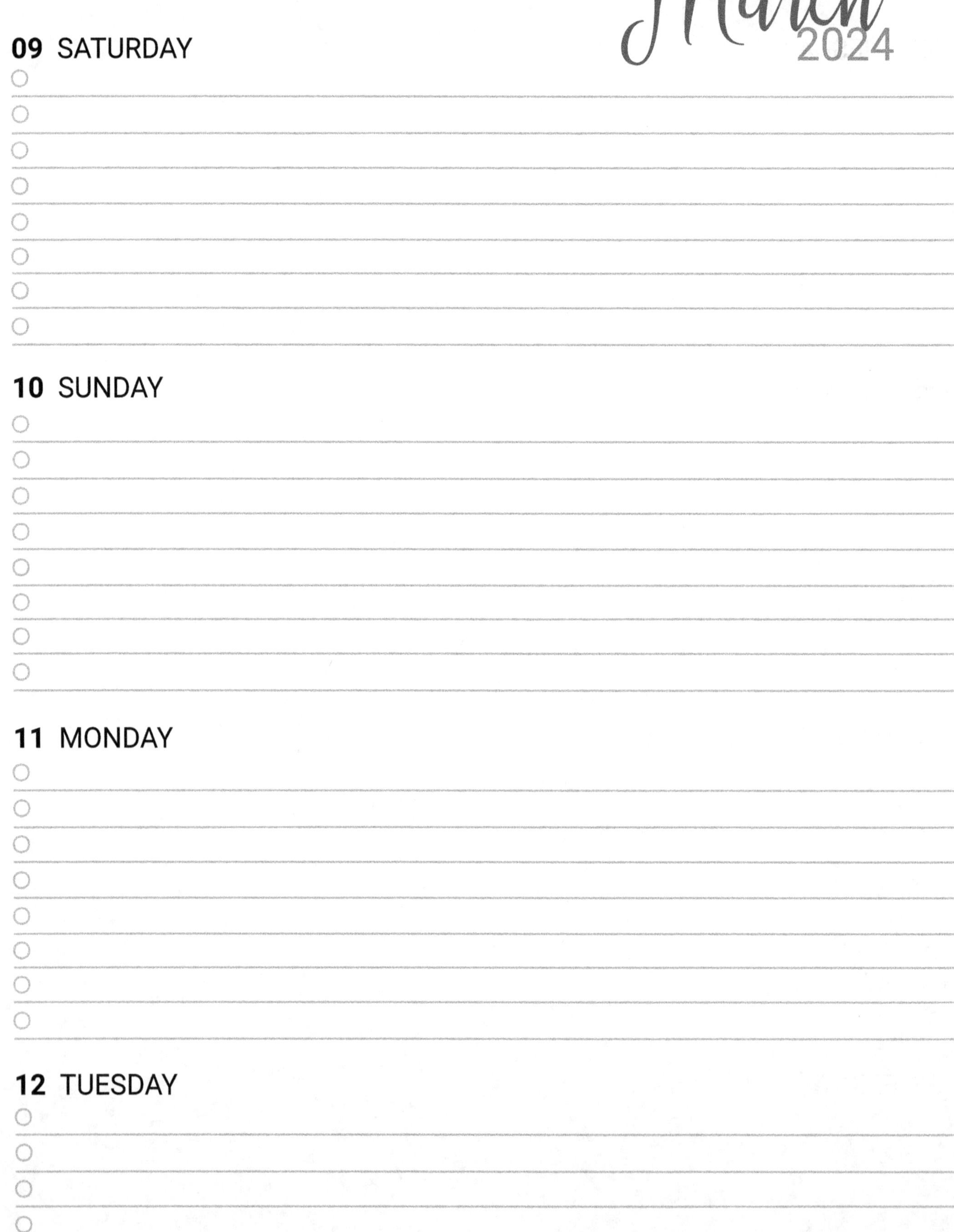

09 SATURDAY

10 SUNDAY

11 MONDAY

12 TUESDAY

March
2024

13 WEDNESDAY

14 THURSDAY

15 FRIDAY

16 SATURDAY

17 SUNDAY

18 MONDAY

19 TUESDAY

20 WEDNESDAY

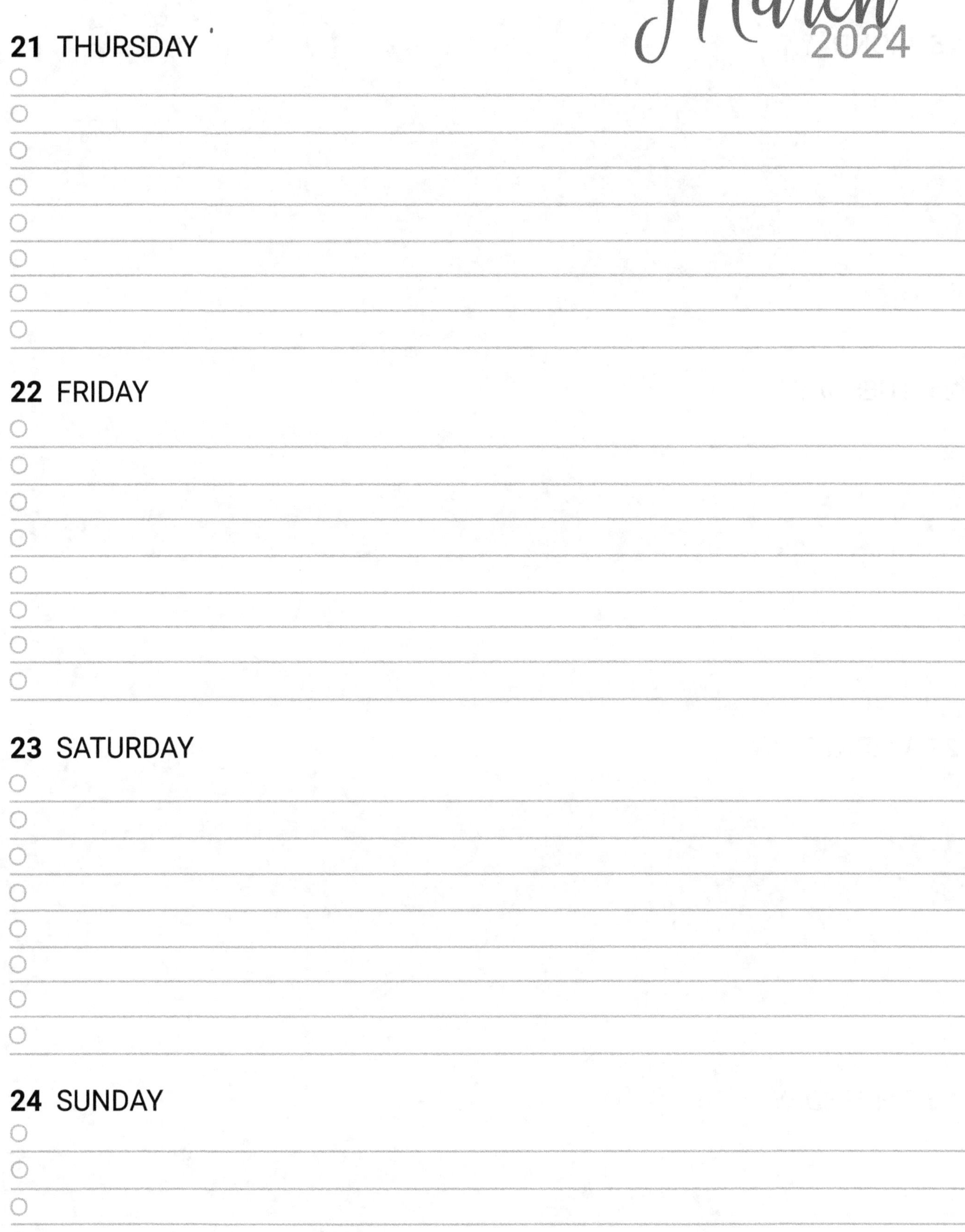

21 THURSDAY

22 FRIDAY

23 SATURDAY

24 SUNDAY

25 MONDAY

26 TUESDAY

27 WEDNESDAY

28 THURSDAY

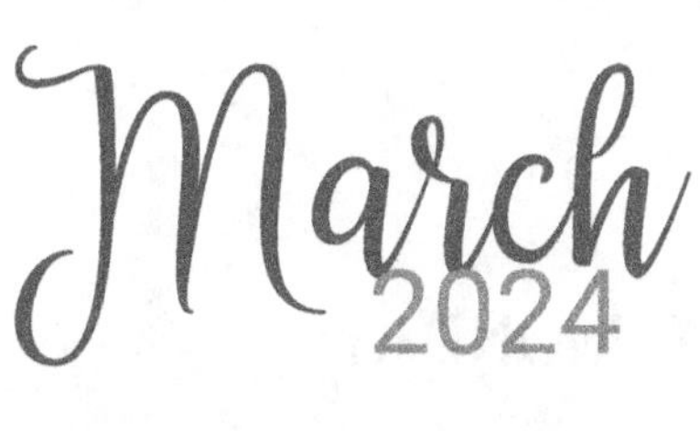

29 FRIDAY

○
○
○
○
○
○
○
○

30 SATURDAY

○
○
○
○
○
○
○
○

31 SUNDAY

○
○
○
○
○
○
○
○

NOTES

01 MONDAY

02 TUESDAY

03 WEDNESDAY

04 THURSDAY

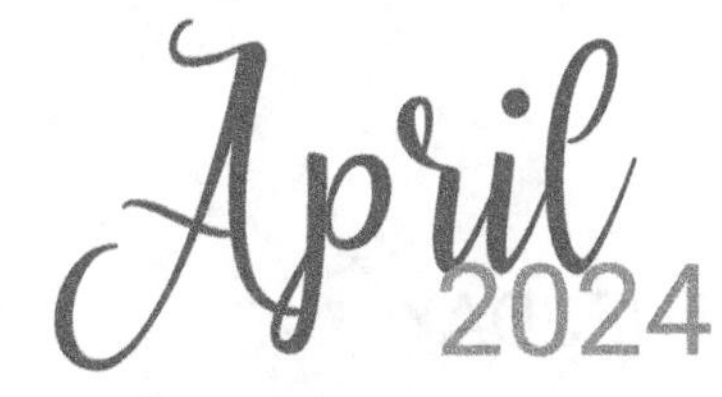

05 FRIDAY

06 SATURDAY

07 SUNDAY

08 MONDAY

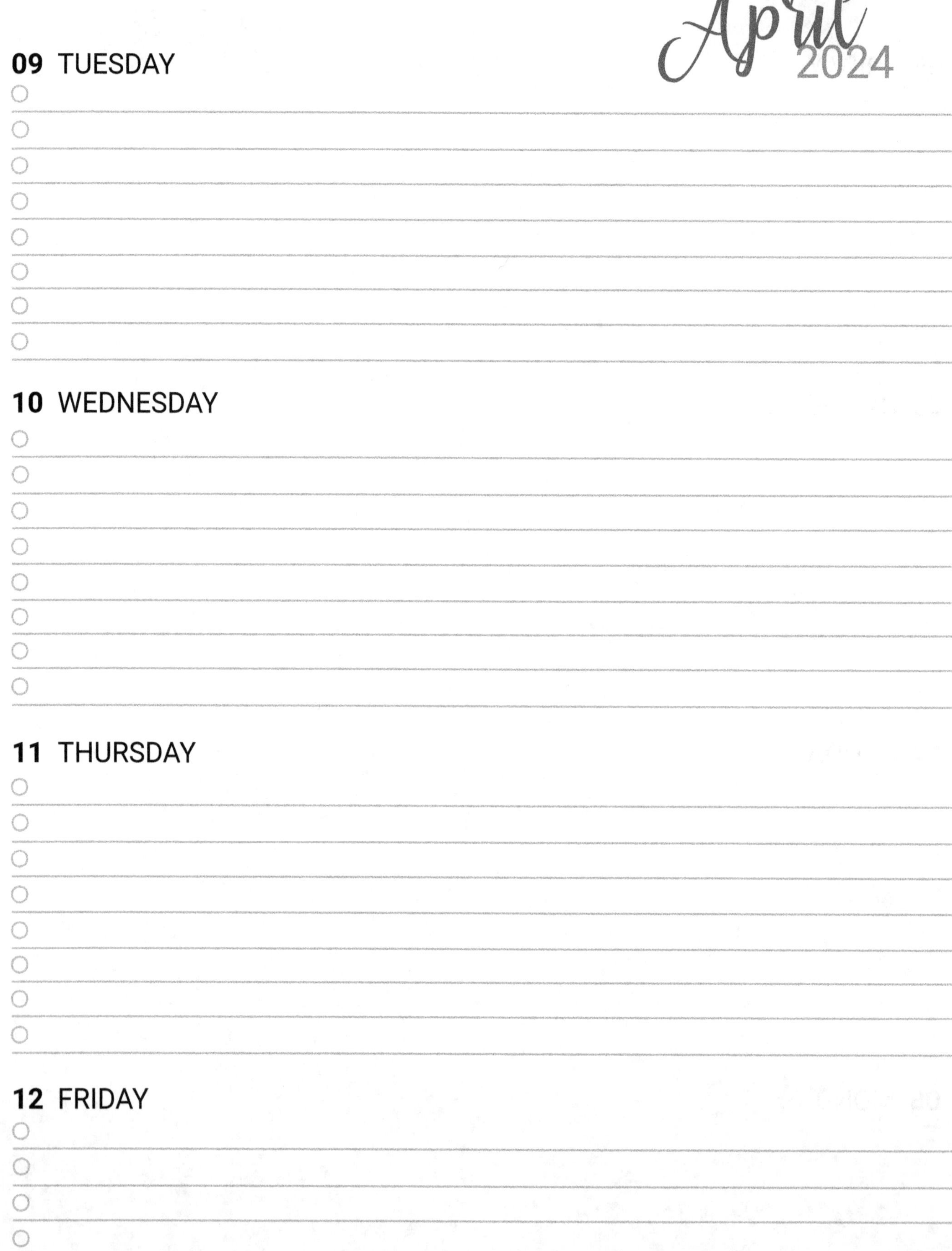

09 TUESDAY

10 WEDNESDAY

11 THURSDAY

12 FRIDAY

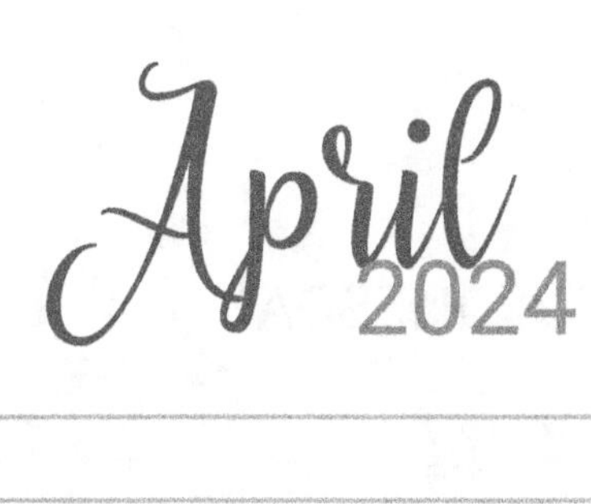

13 SATURDAY

14 SUNDAY

15 MONDAY

16 TUESDAY

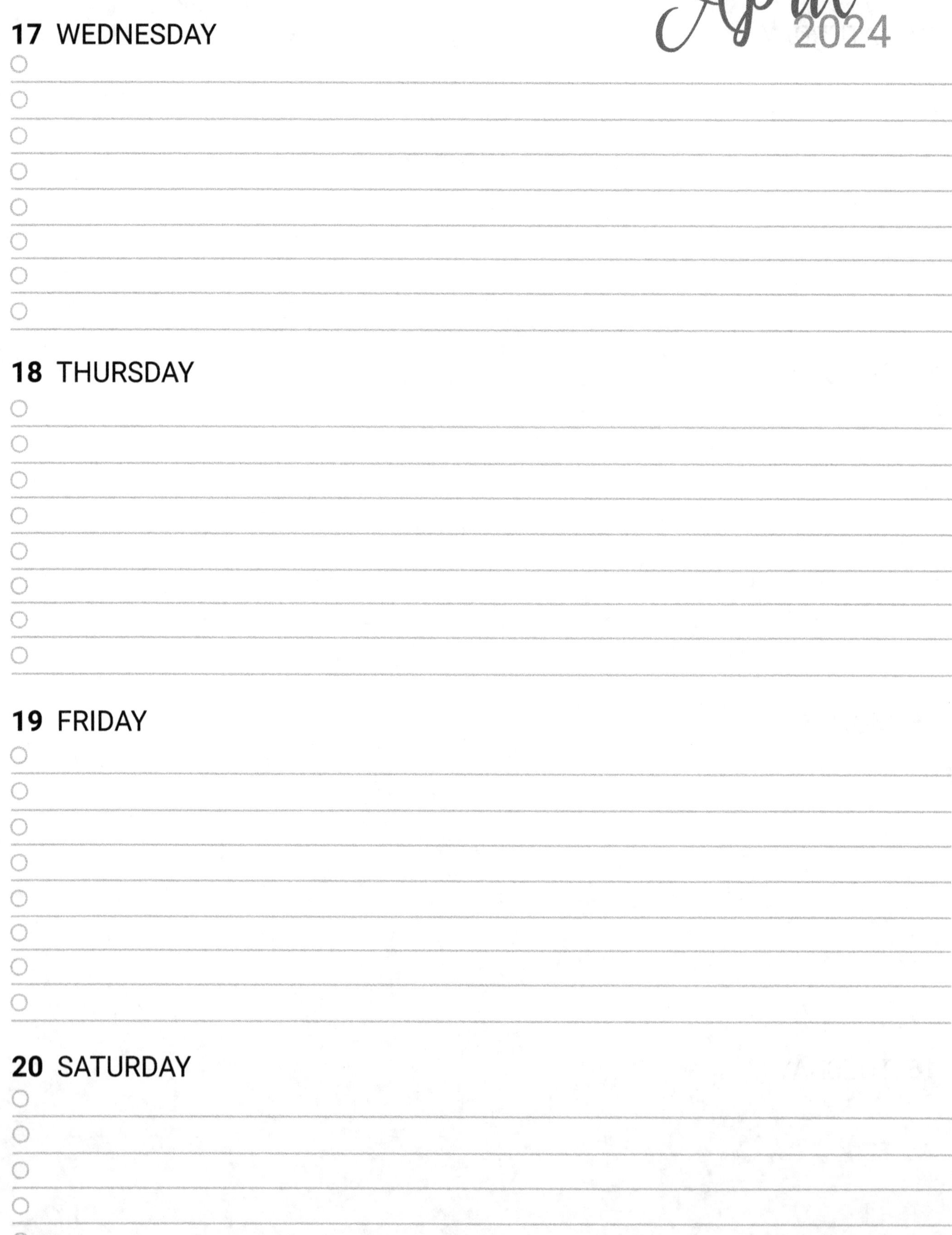

17 WEDNESDAY

18 THURSDAY

19 FRIDAY

20 SATURDAY

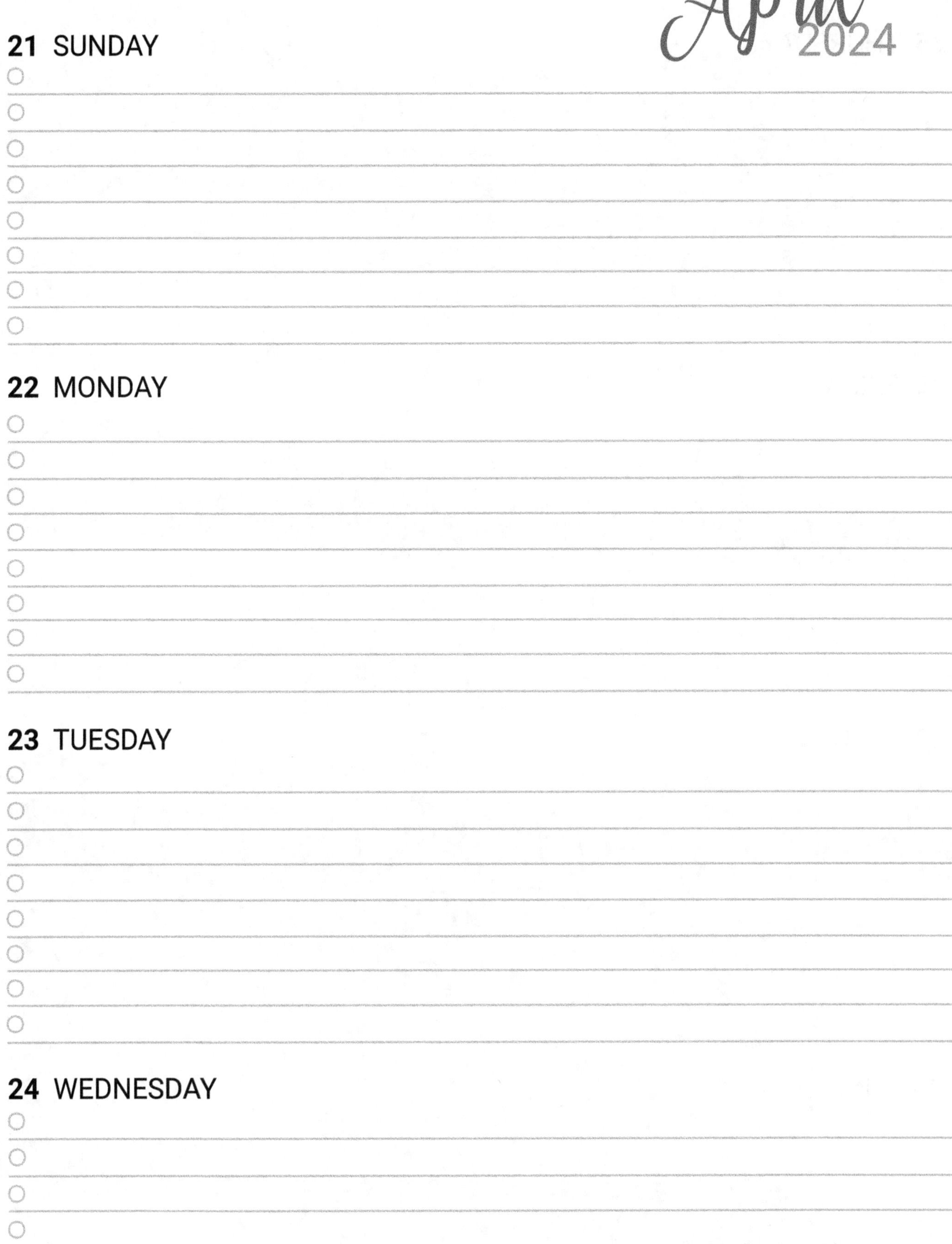

21 SUNDAY

22 MONDAY

23 TUESDAY

24 WEDNESDAY

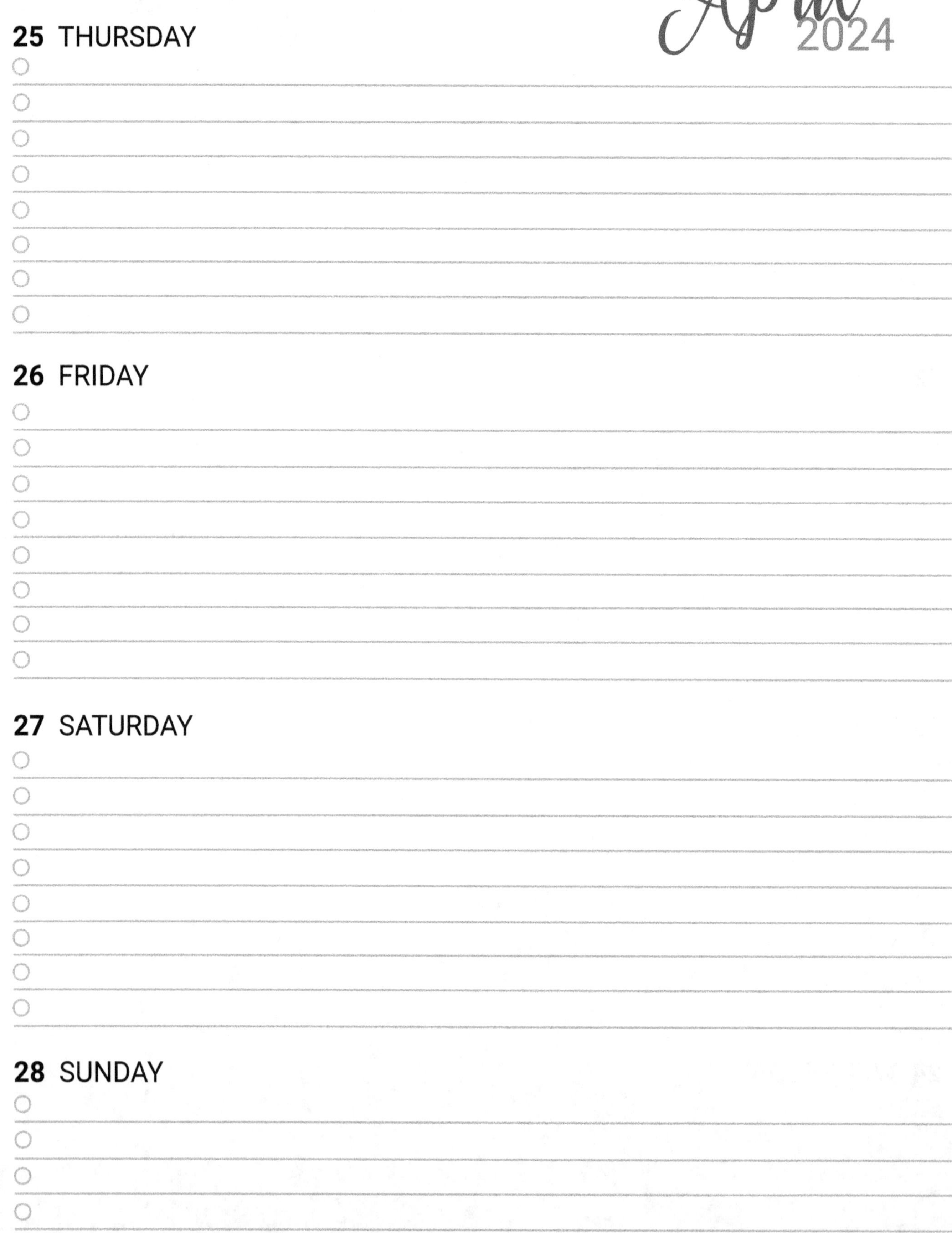

25 THURSDAY

26 FRIDAY

27 SATURDAY

28 SUNDAY

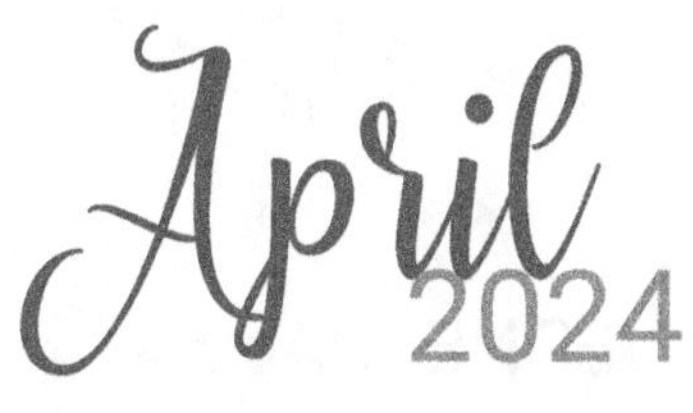

29 MONDAY

30 TUESDAY

NOTES

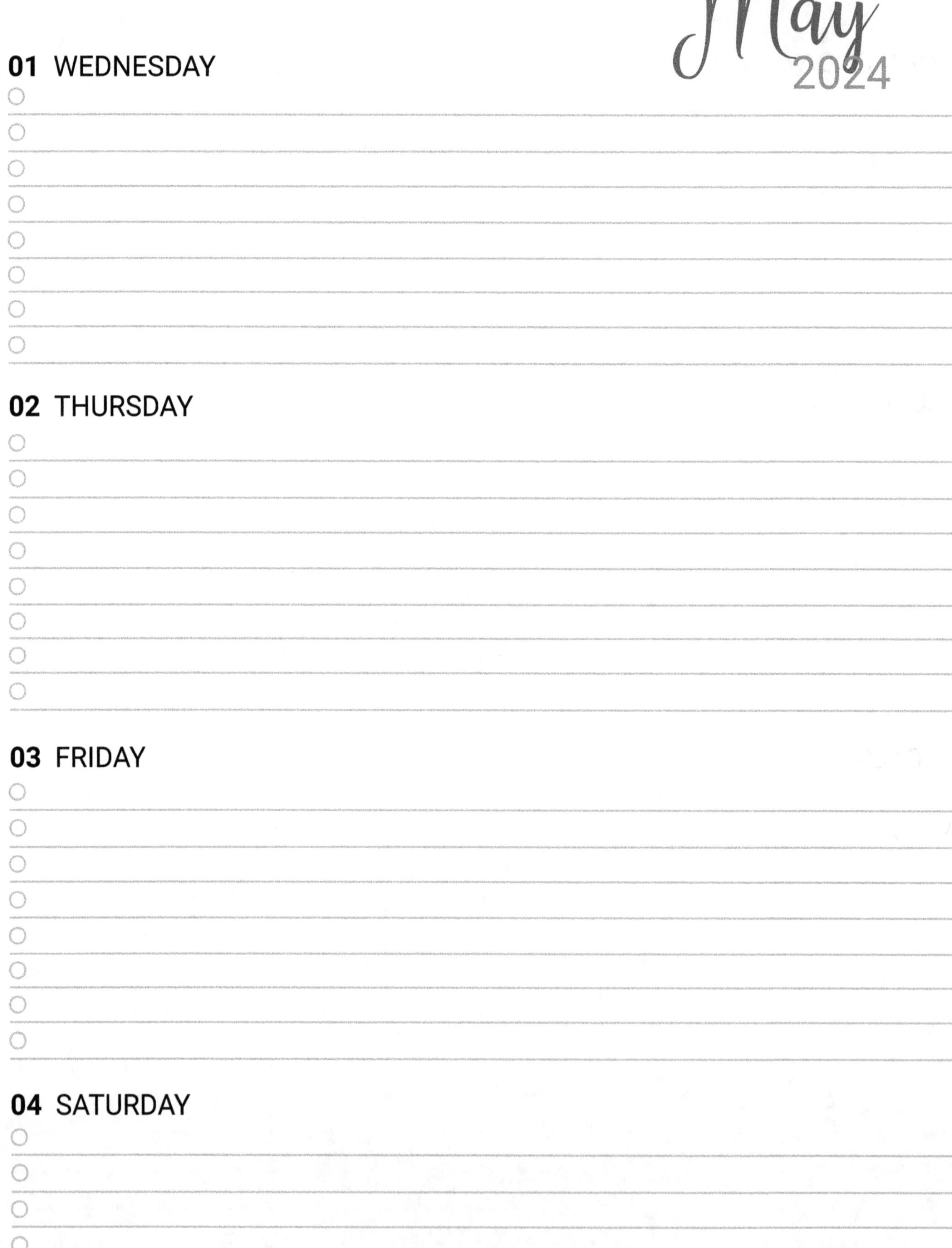

May 2024

01 WEDNESDAY

02 THURSDAY

03 FRIDAY

04 SATURDAY

May
2024

05 SUNDAY

06 MONDAY

07 TUESDAY

08 WEDNESDAY

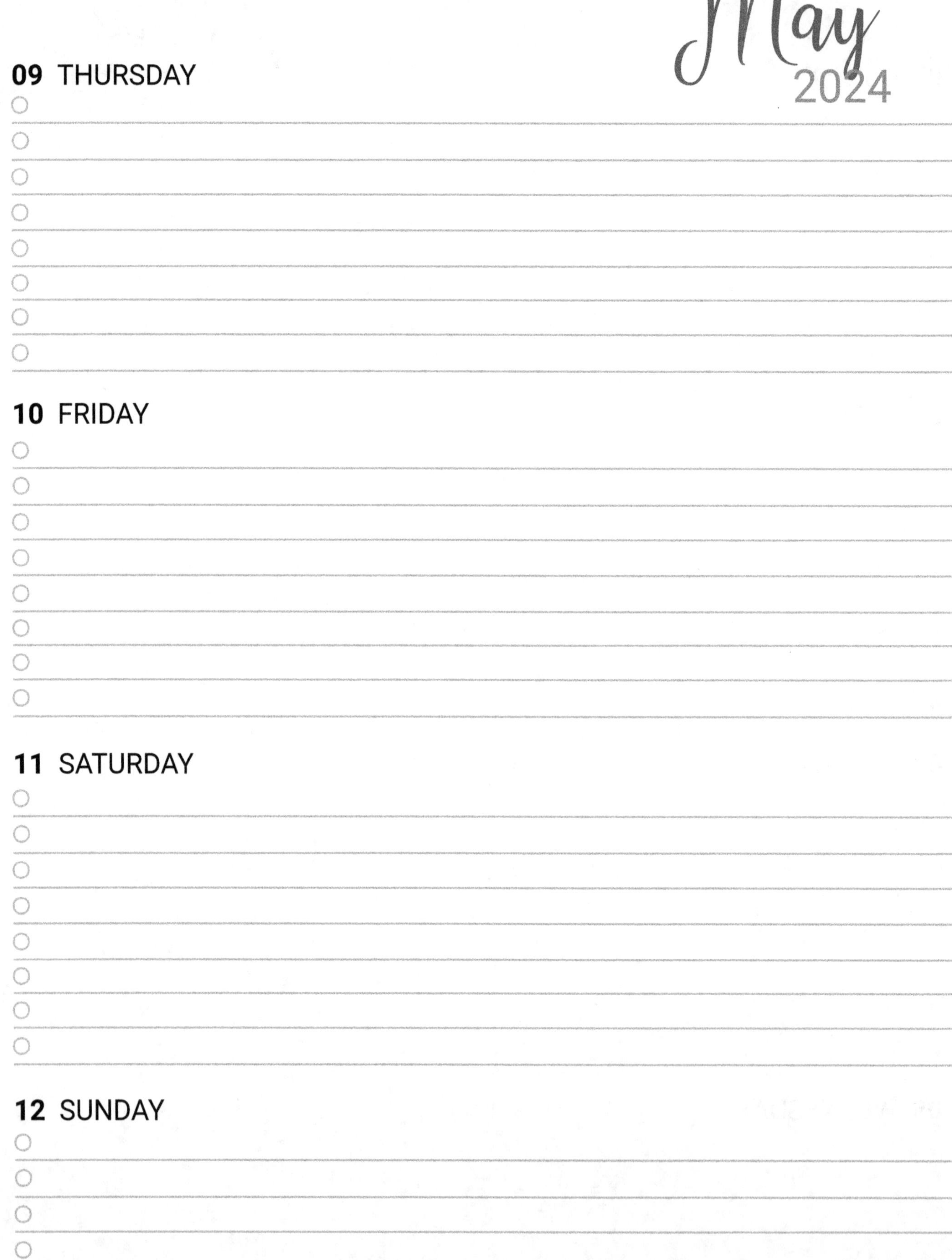

May
2024

09 THURSDAY

10 FRIDAY

11 SATURDAY

12 SUNDAY

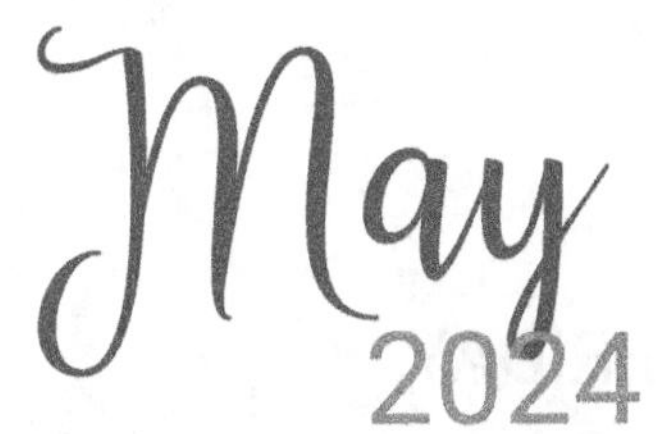

13 MONDAY

○
○
○
○
○
○
○
○

14 TUESDAY

○
○
○
○
○
○
○
○

15 WEDNESDAY

○
○
○
○
○
○
○
○

16 THURSDAY

○
○
○
○
○

May
2024

17 FRIDAY

18 SATURDAY

19 SUNDAY

20 MONDAY

May
2024

21 TUESDAY

22 WEDNESDAY

23 THURSDAY

24 FRIDAY

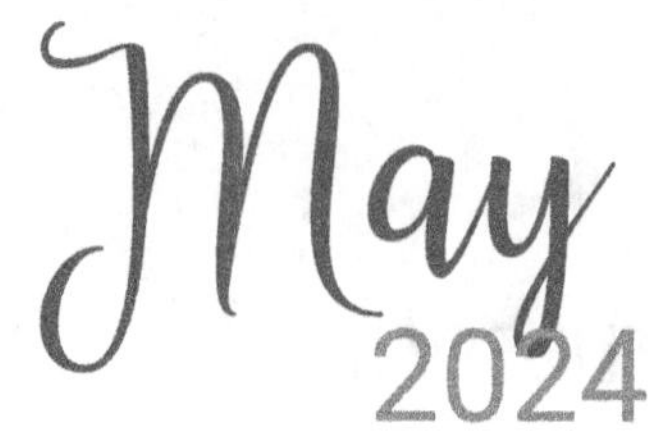

25 SATURDAY

26 SUNDAY

27 MONDAY

28 TUESDAY

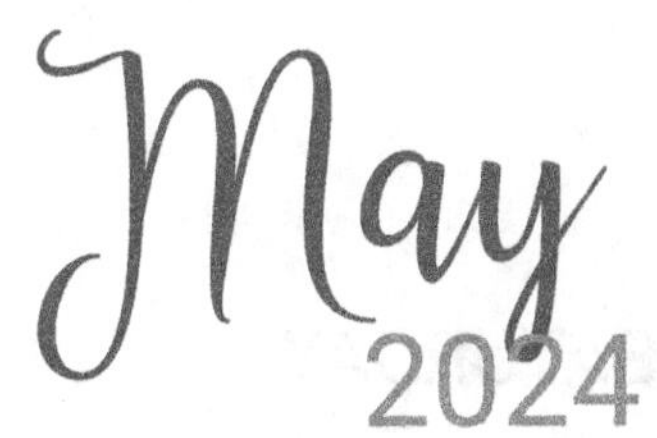

29 WEDNESDAY

30 THURSDAY

31 FRIDAY

NOTES

June
2024

01 SATURDAY

02 SUNDAY

03 MONDAY

04 TUESDAY

05 WEDNESDAY

06 THURSDAY

07 FRIDAY

08 SATURDAY

09 SUNDAY

10 MONDAY

11 TUESDAY

12 WEDNESDAY

13 THURSDAY

14 FRIDAY

15 SATURDAY

16 SUNDAY

17 MONDAY

18 TUESDAY

19 WEDNESDAY

20 THURSDAY

21 FRIDAY

22 SATURDAY

23 SUNDAY

24 MONDAY

25 TUESDAY

26 WEDNESDAY

27 THURSDAY

28 FRIDAY

29 SATURDAY

30 SUNDAY

NOTES

01 MONDAY

02 TUESDAY

03 WEDNESDAY

04 THURSDAY

July
2024

05 FRIDAY

- ◯
- ◯
- ◯
- ◯
- ◯
- ◯
- ◯
- ◯

06 SATURDAY

- ◯
- ◯
- ◯
- ◯
- ◯
- ◯
- ◯
- ◯

07 SUNDAY

- ◯
- ◯
- ◯
- ◯
- ◯
- ◯
- ◯
- ◯

08 MONDAY

- ◯
- ◯
- ◯
- ◯
- ◯

09 TUESDAY

10 WEDNESDAY

11 THURSDAY

12 FRIDAY

13 SATURDAY

14 SUNDAY

15 MONDAY

16 TUESDAY

17 WEDNESDAY

18 THURSDAY

19 FRIDAY

20 SATURDAY

21 SUNDAY

22 MONDAY

23 TUESDAY

24 WEDNESDAY

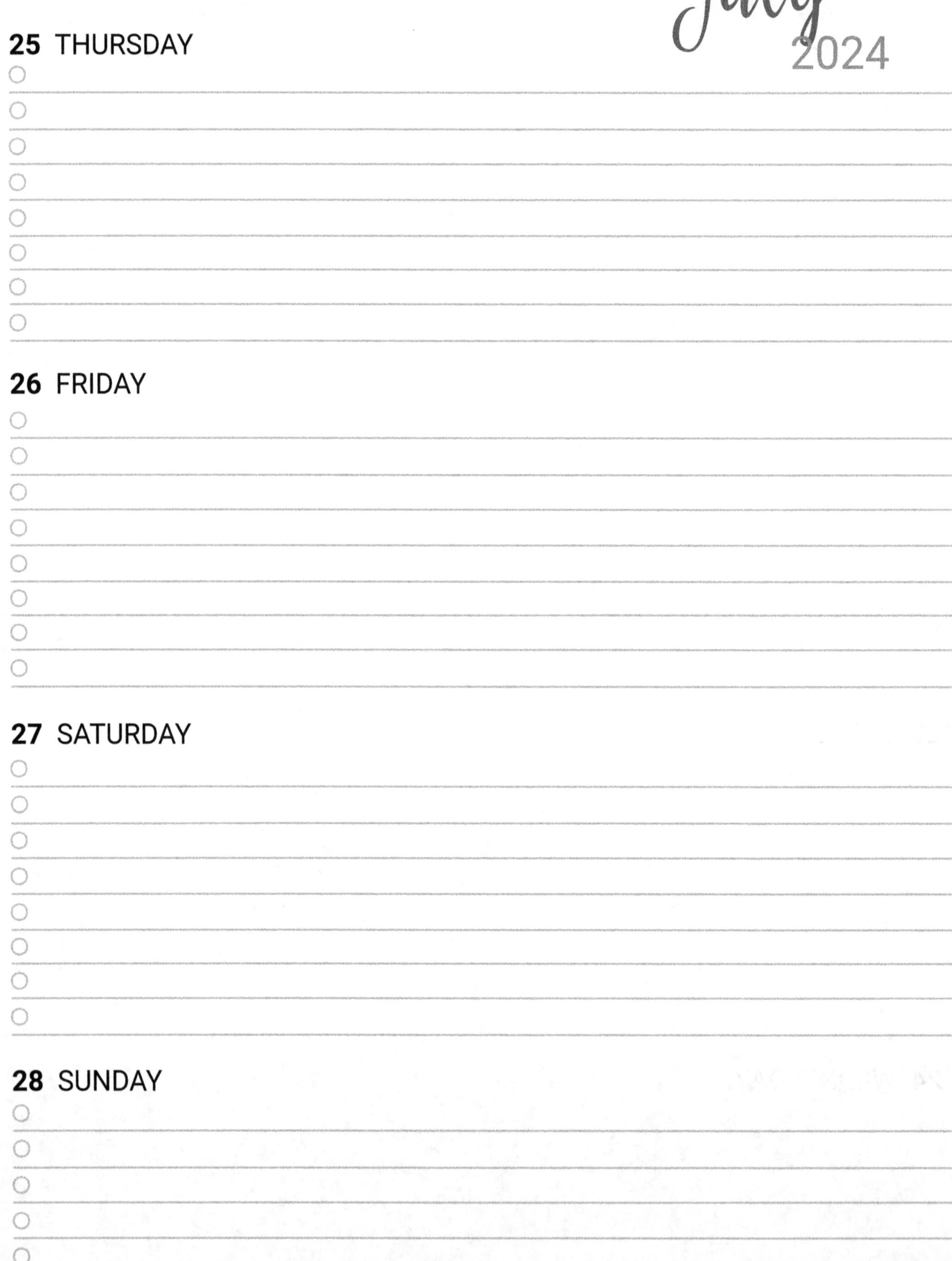

July
2024

25 THURSDAY

26 FRIDAY

27 SATURDAY

28 SUNDAY

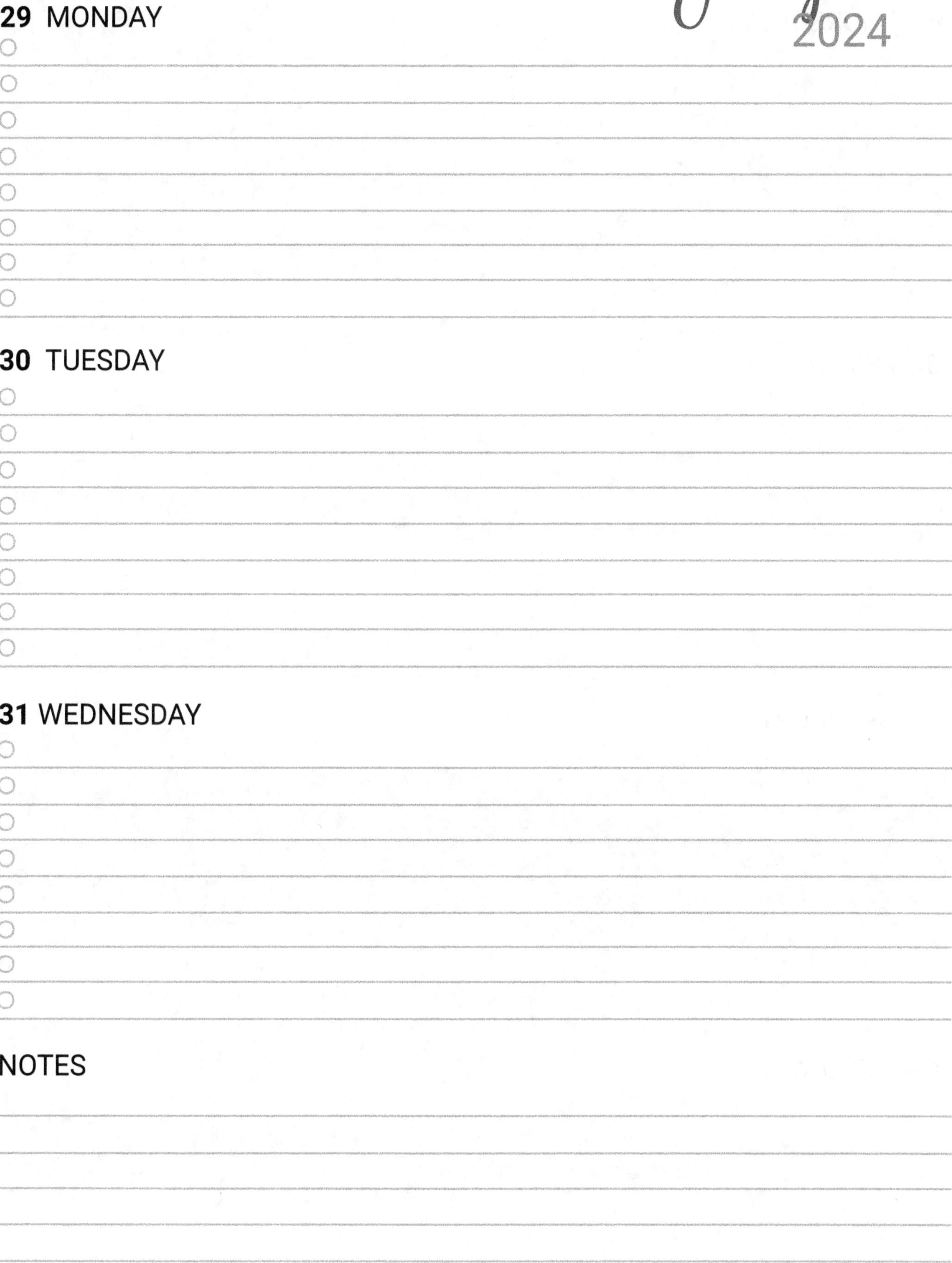

29 MONDAY

30 TUESDAY

31 WEDNESDAY

NOTES

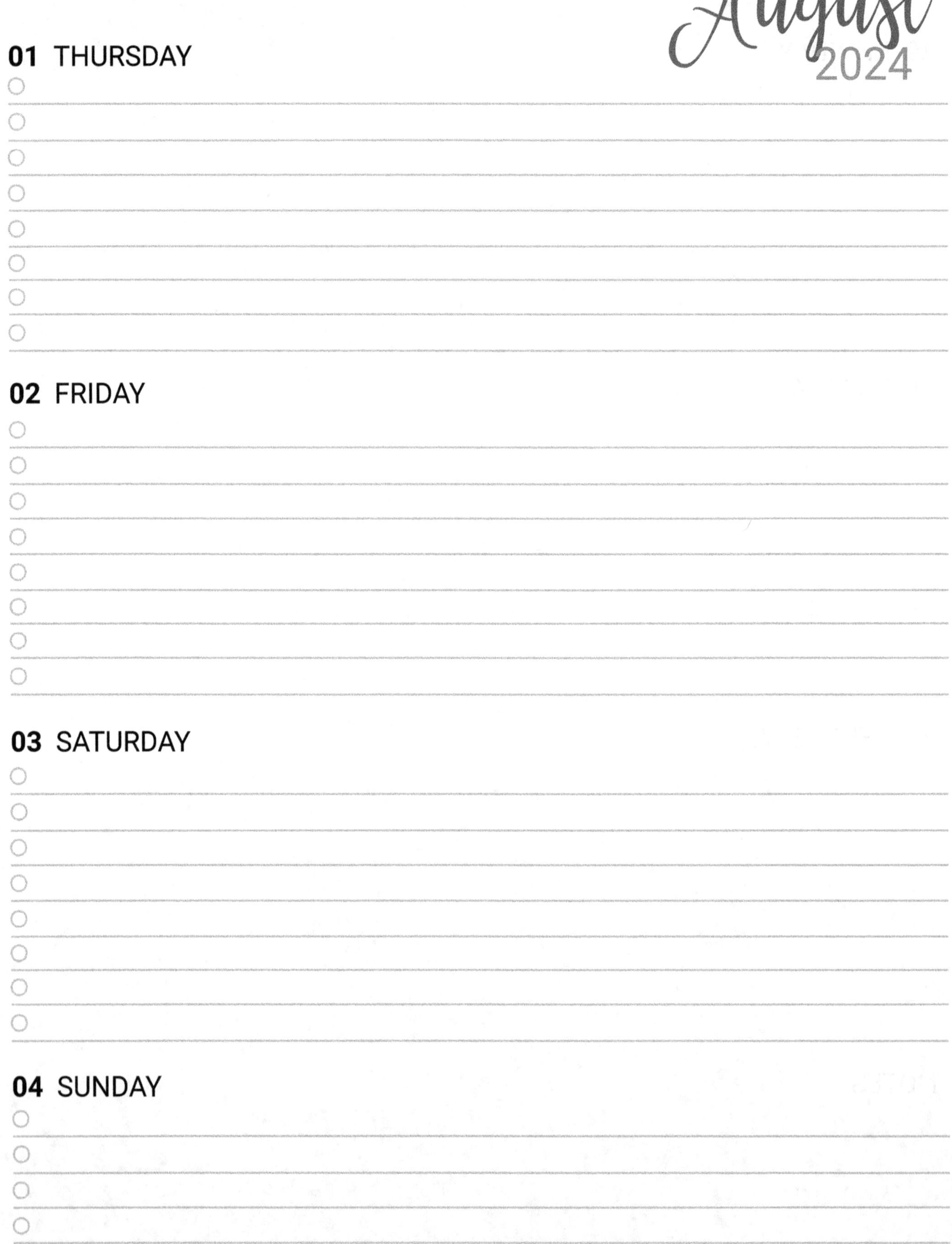

<h1>August</h1>2024

01 THURSDAY

02 FRIDAY

03 SATURDAY

04 SUNDAY

05 MONDAY

06 TUESDAY

07 WEDNESDAY

08 THURSDAY

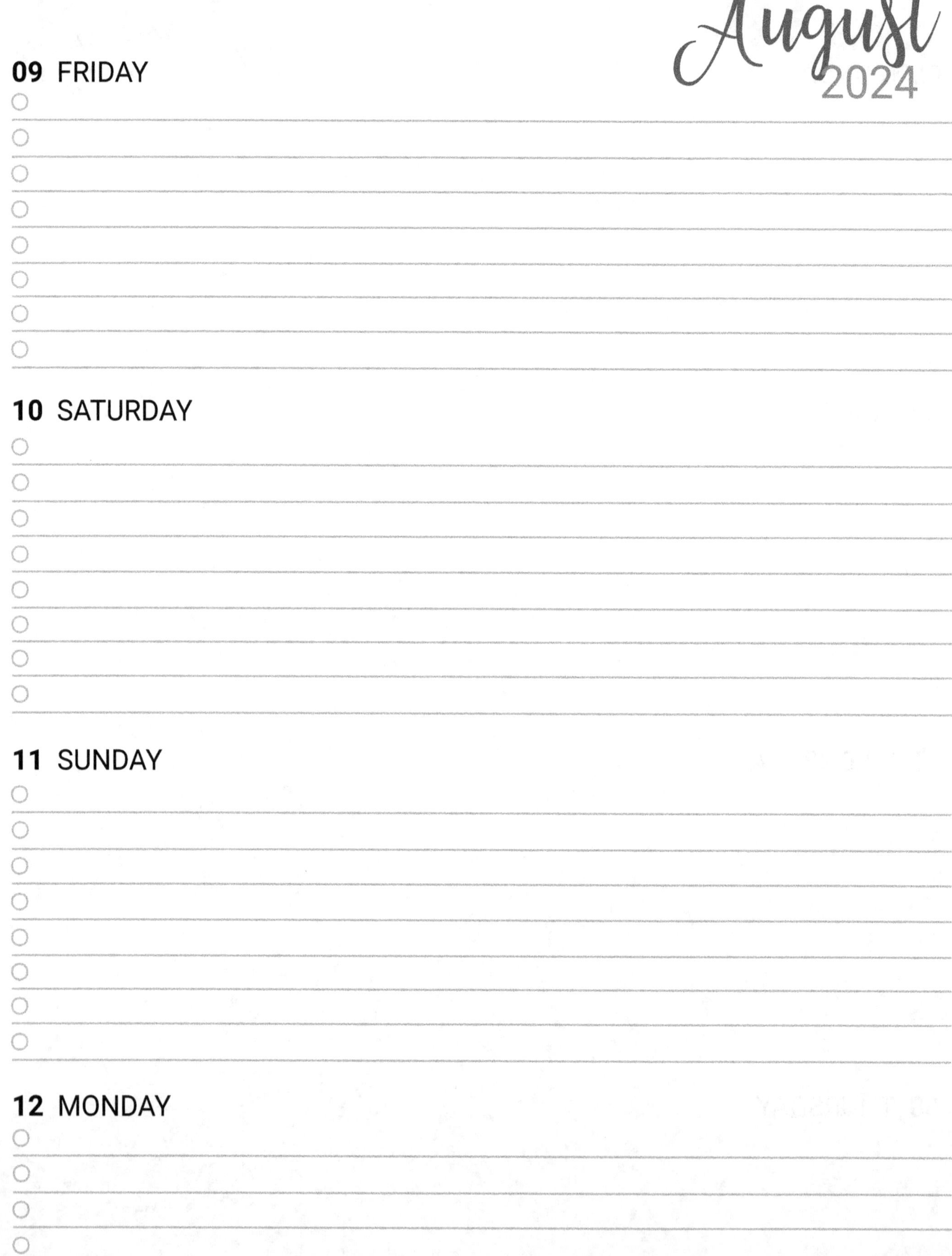

August
2024

09 FRIDAY

10 SATURDAY

11 SUNDAY

12 MONDAY

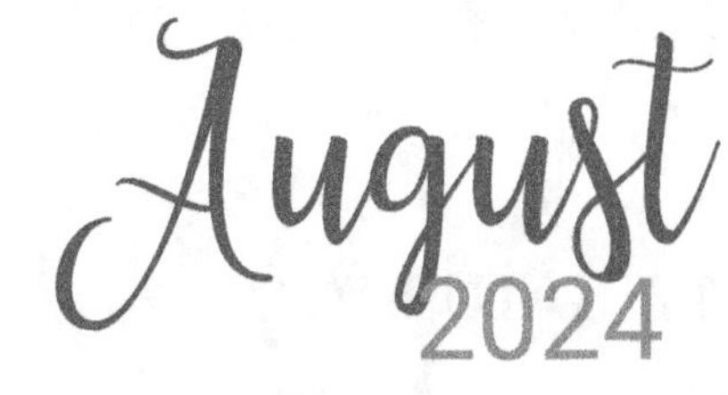

13 TUESDAY

14 WEDNESDAY

15 THURSDAY

16 FRIDAY

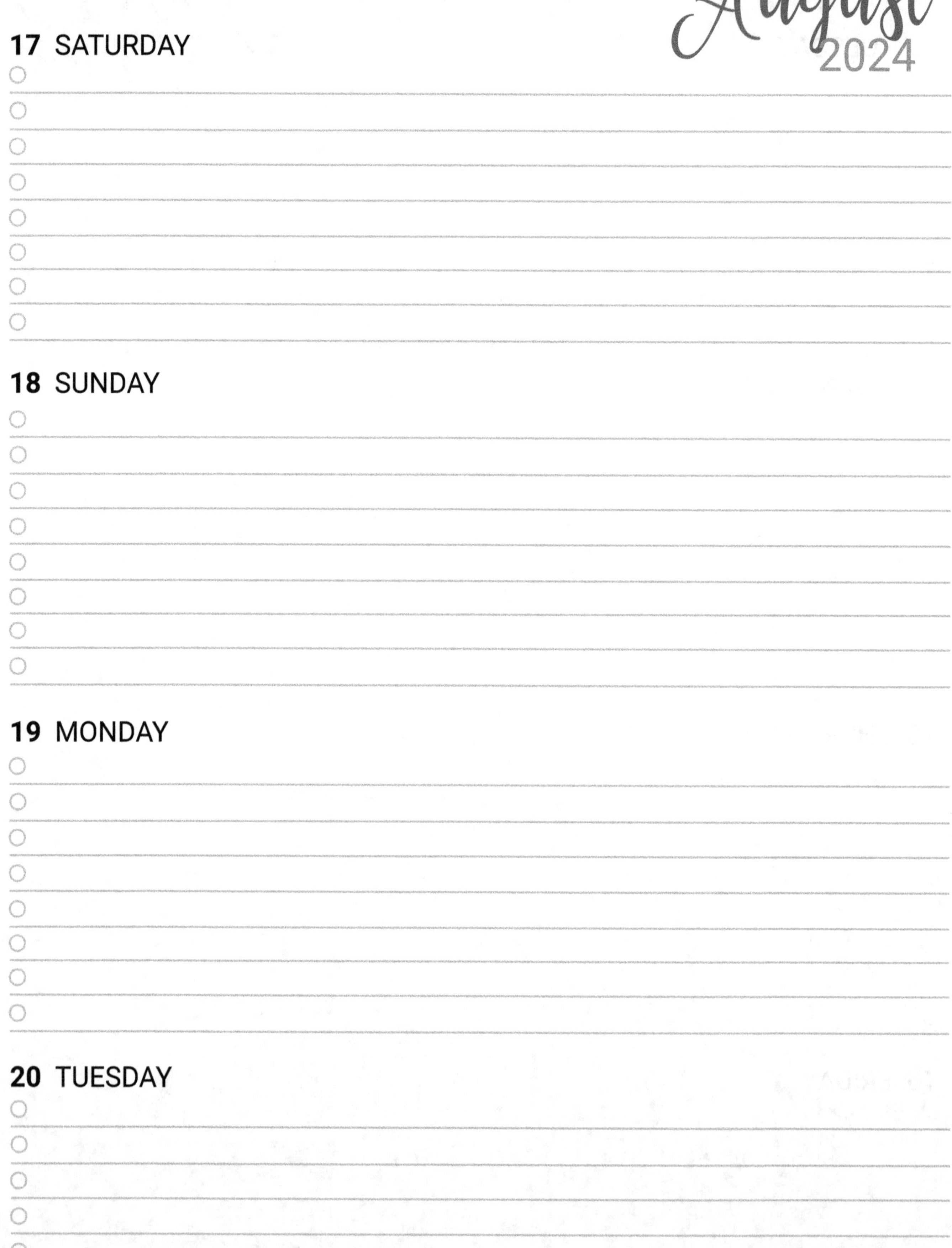

17 SATURDAY

18 SUNDAY

19 MONDAY

20 TUESDAY

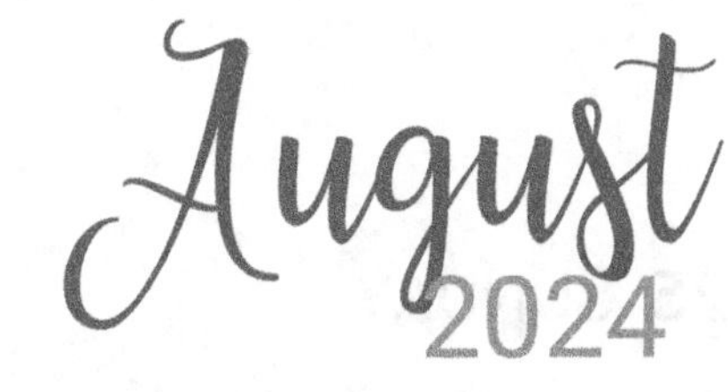

August
2024

21 WEDNESDAY

22 THURSDAY

23 FRIDAY

24 SATURDAY

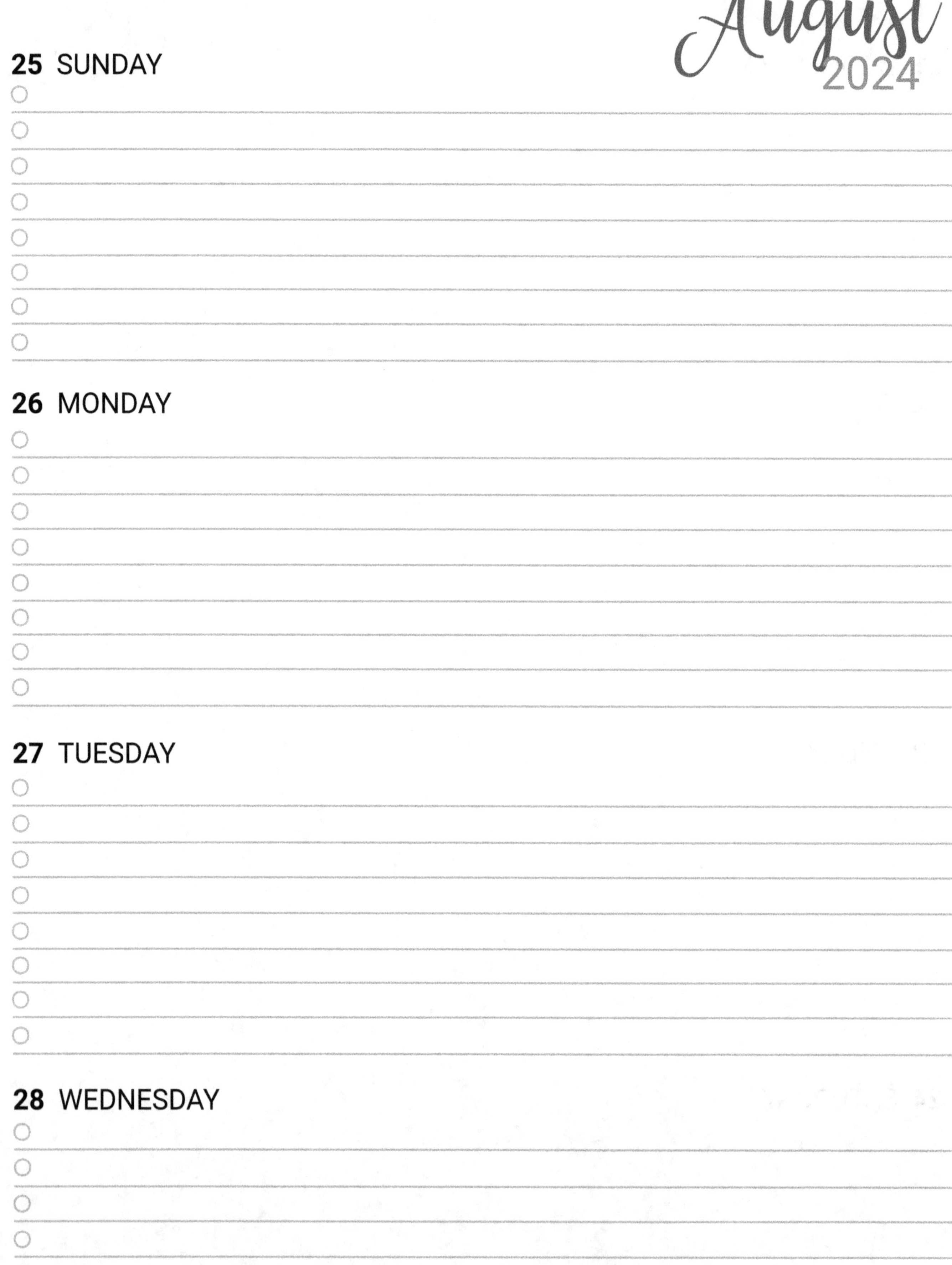

25 SUNDAY

26 MONDAY

27 TUESDAY

28 WEDNESDAY

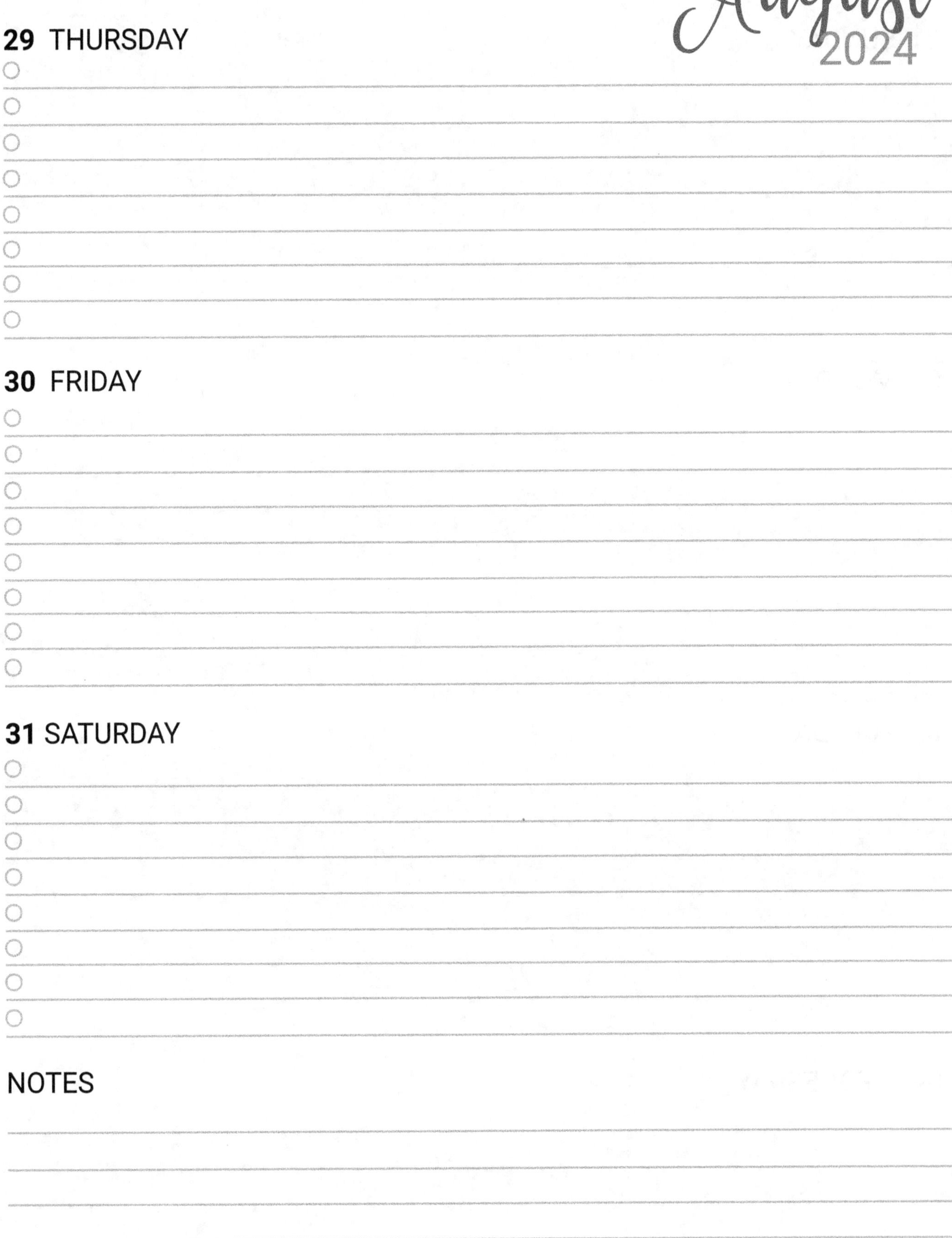

August
2024

29 THURSDAY

30 FRIDAY

31 SATURDAY

NOTES

01 SUNDAY

02 MONDAY

03 TUESDAY

04 WEDNESDAY

05 THURSDAY

- ○
- ○
- ○
- ○
- ○
- ○
- ○
- ○

06 FRIDAY

- ○
- ○
- ○
- ○
- ○
- ○
- ○
- ○

07 SATURDAY

- ○
- ○
- ○
- ○
- ○
- ○
- ○
- ○

08 SUNDAY

- ○
- ○
- ○
- ○
- ○

09 MONDAY

10 TUESDAY

11 WEDNESDAY

12 THURSDAY

13 FRIDAY

14 SATURDAY

15 SUNDAY

16 MONDAY

17 TUESDAY

18 WEDNESDAY

19 THURSDAY

20 FRIDAY

21 SATURDAY

22 SUNDAY

23 MONDAY

24 TUESDAY

25 WEDNESDAY

26 THURSDAY

27 FRIDAY

28 SATURDAY

September
2024

29 SUNDAY

- ○
- ○
- ○
- ○
- ○
- ○
- ○
- ○

30 MONDAY

- ○
- ○
- ○
- ○
- ○
- ○
- ○
- ○

NOTES

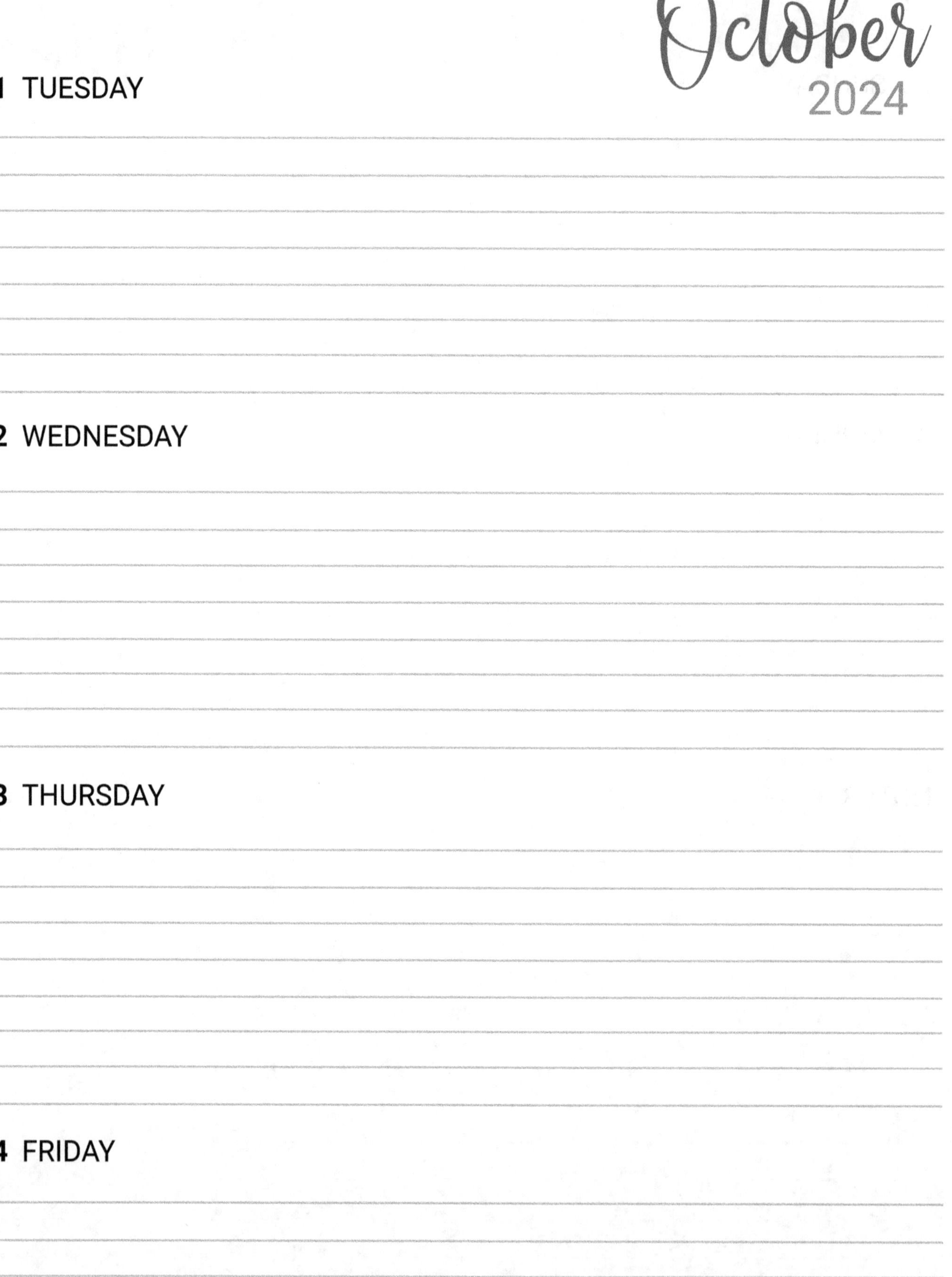

October
2024

01 TUESDAY

02 WEDNESDAY

03 THURSDAY

04 FRIDAY

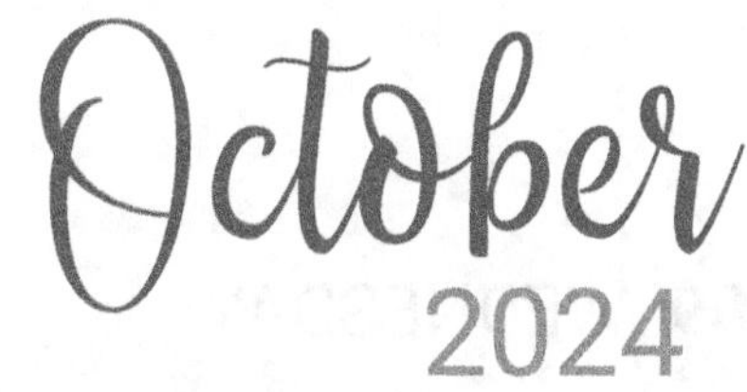

05 SATURDAY

○
○
○
○
○
○
○
○

06 SUNDAY

○
○
○
○
○
○
○
○

07 MONDAY

○
○
○
○
○
○
○
○

08 TUESDAY

○
○
○
○
○

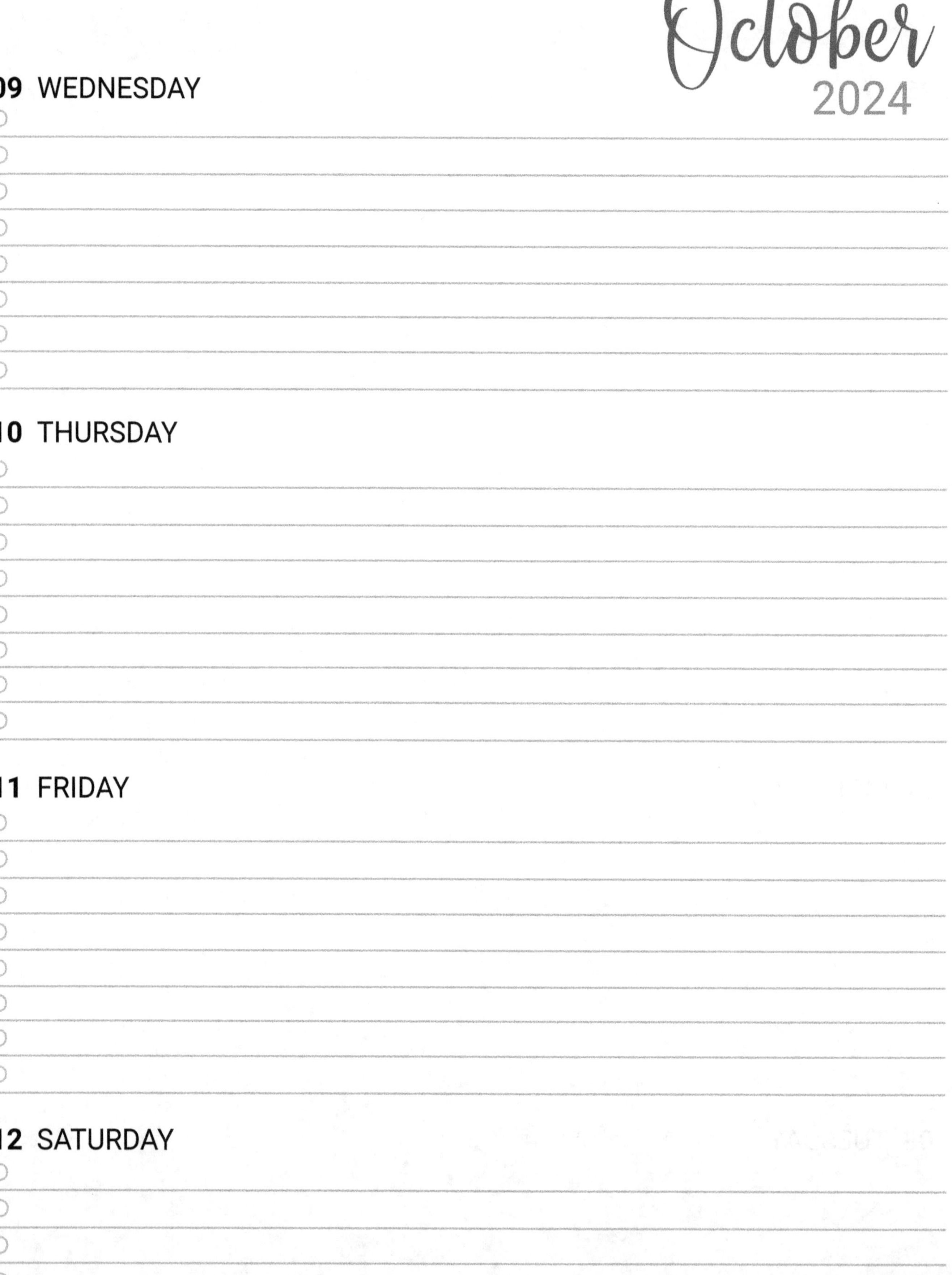

09 WEDNESDAY

10 THURSDAY

11 FRIDAY

12 SATURDAY

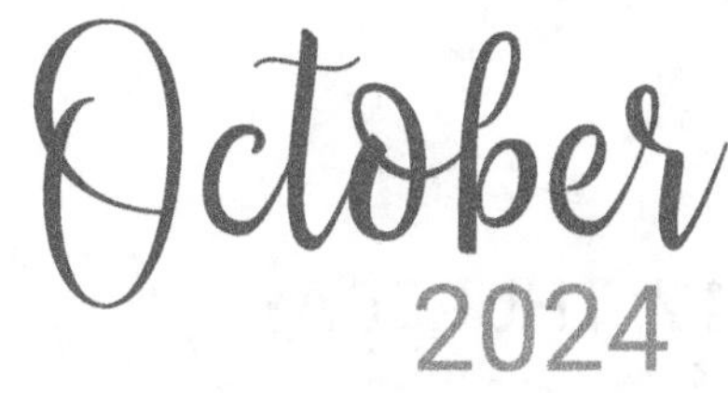

13 SUNDAY

14 MONDAY

15 TUESDAY

16 WEDNESDAY

17 THURSDAY

18 FRIDAY

19 SATURDAY

20 SUNDAY

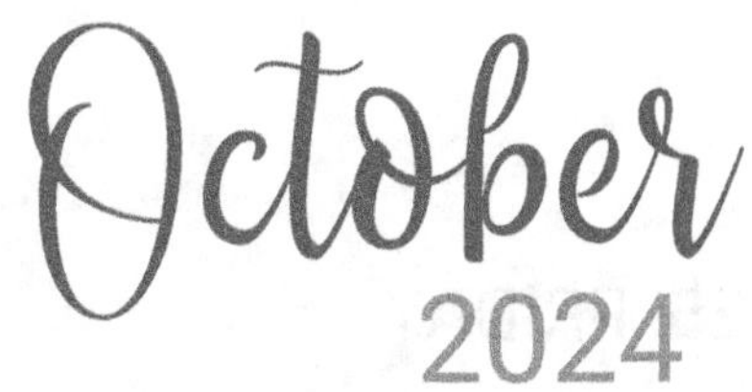

October
2024

21 MONDAY

22 TUESDAY

23 WEDNESDAY

24 THURSDAY

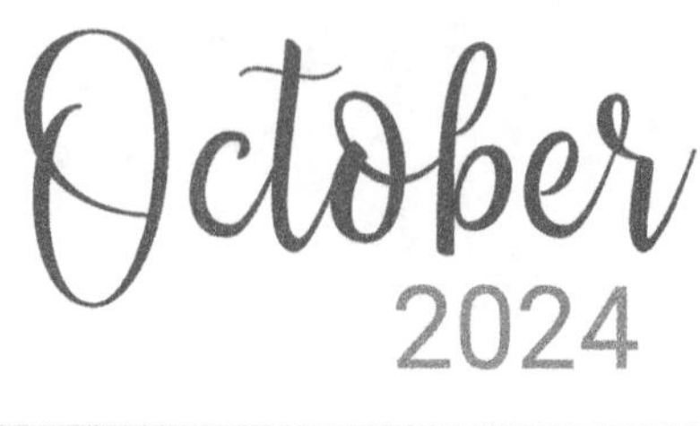

25 FRIDAY

26 SATURDAY

27 SUNDAY

28 MONDAY

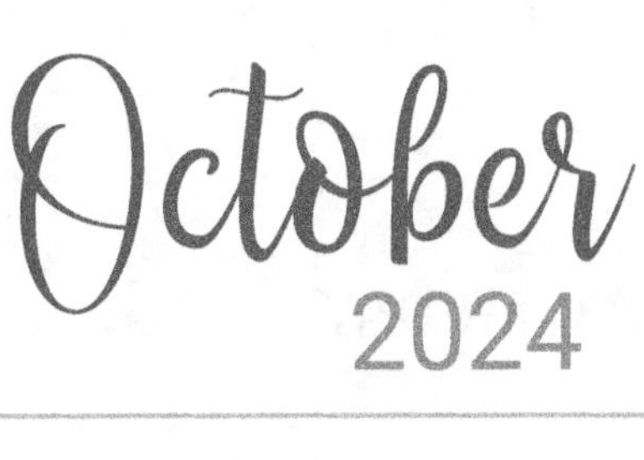

29 TUESDAY

30 WEDNESDAY

31 THURSDAY

NOTES

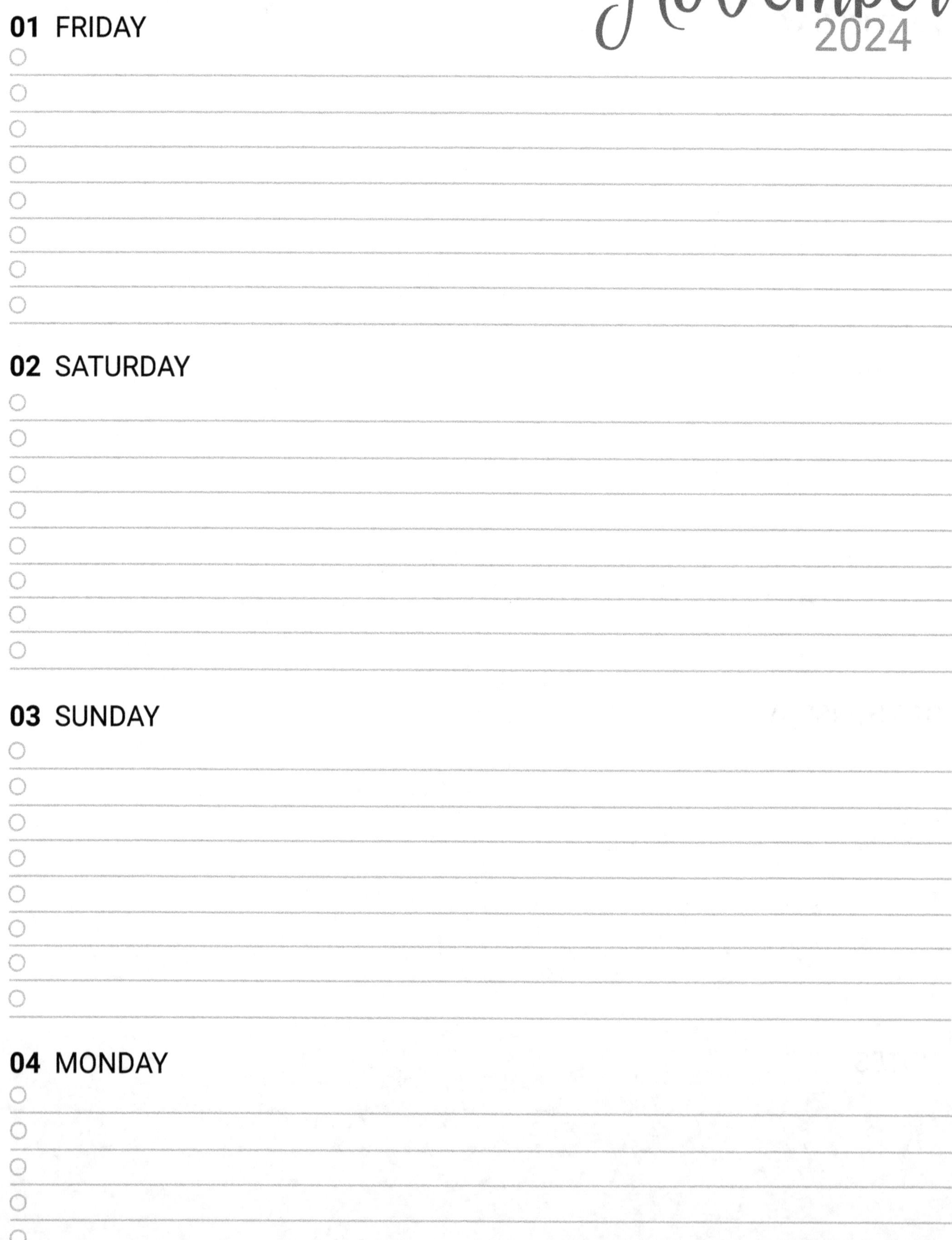

November
2024

01 FRIDAY

02 SATURDAY

03 SUNDAY

04 MONDAY

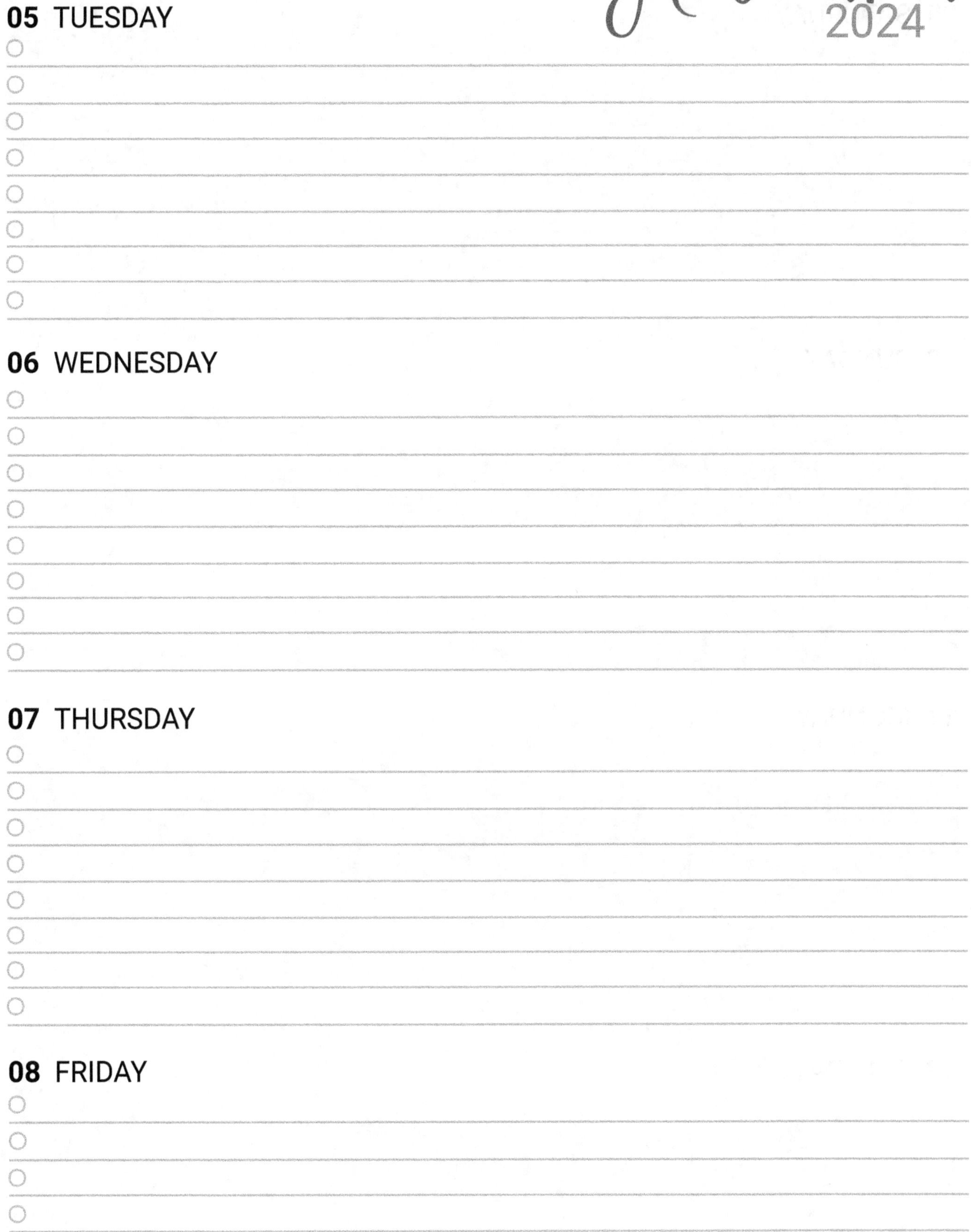

November
2024

05 TUESDAY

06 WEDNESDAY

07 THURSDAY

08 FRIDAY

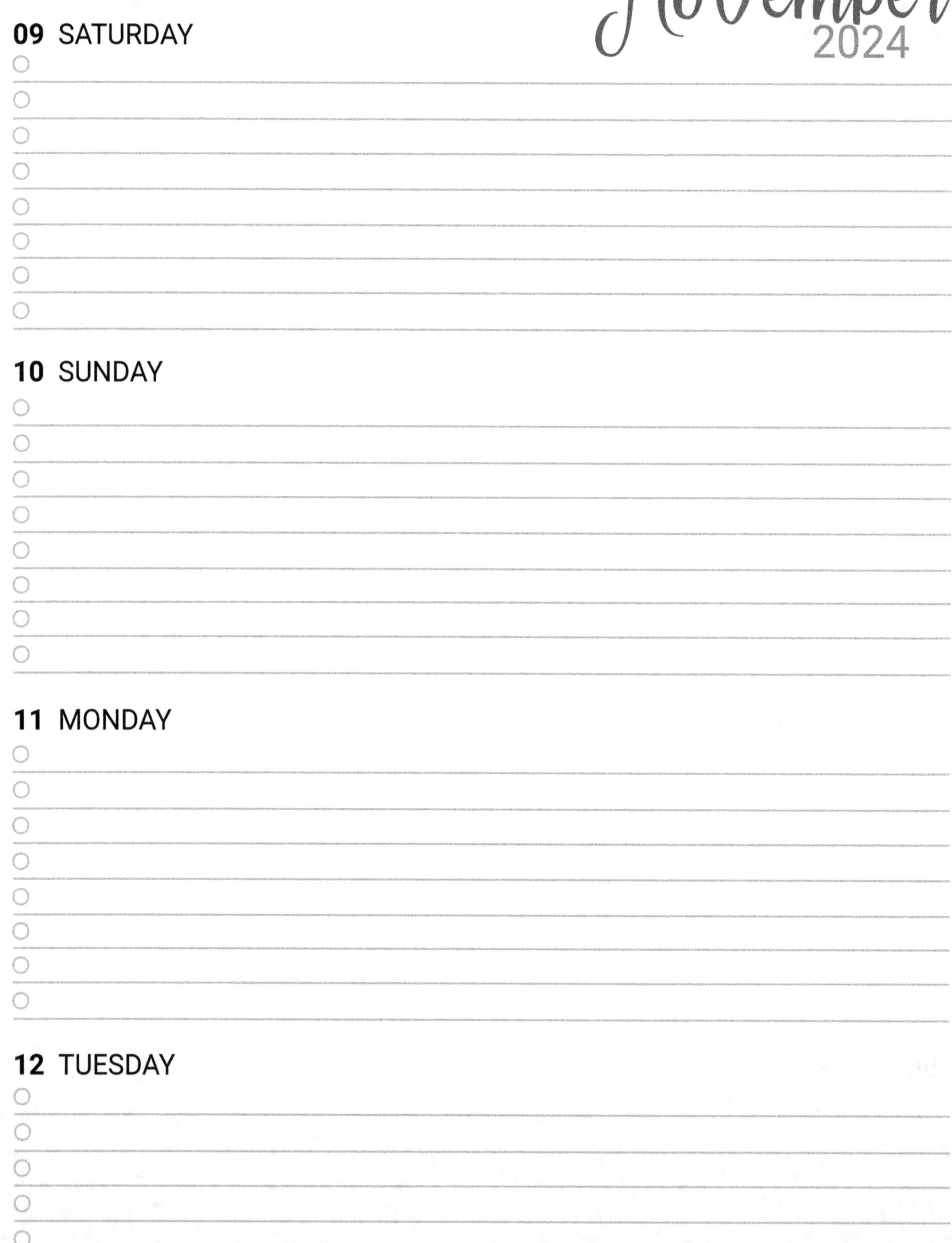

09 SATURDAY

10 SUNDAY

11 MONDAY

12 TUESDAY

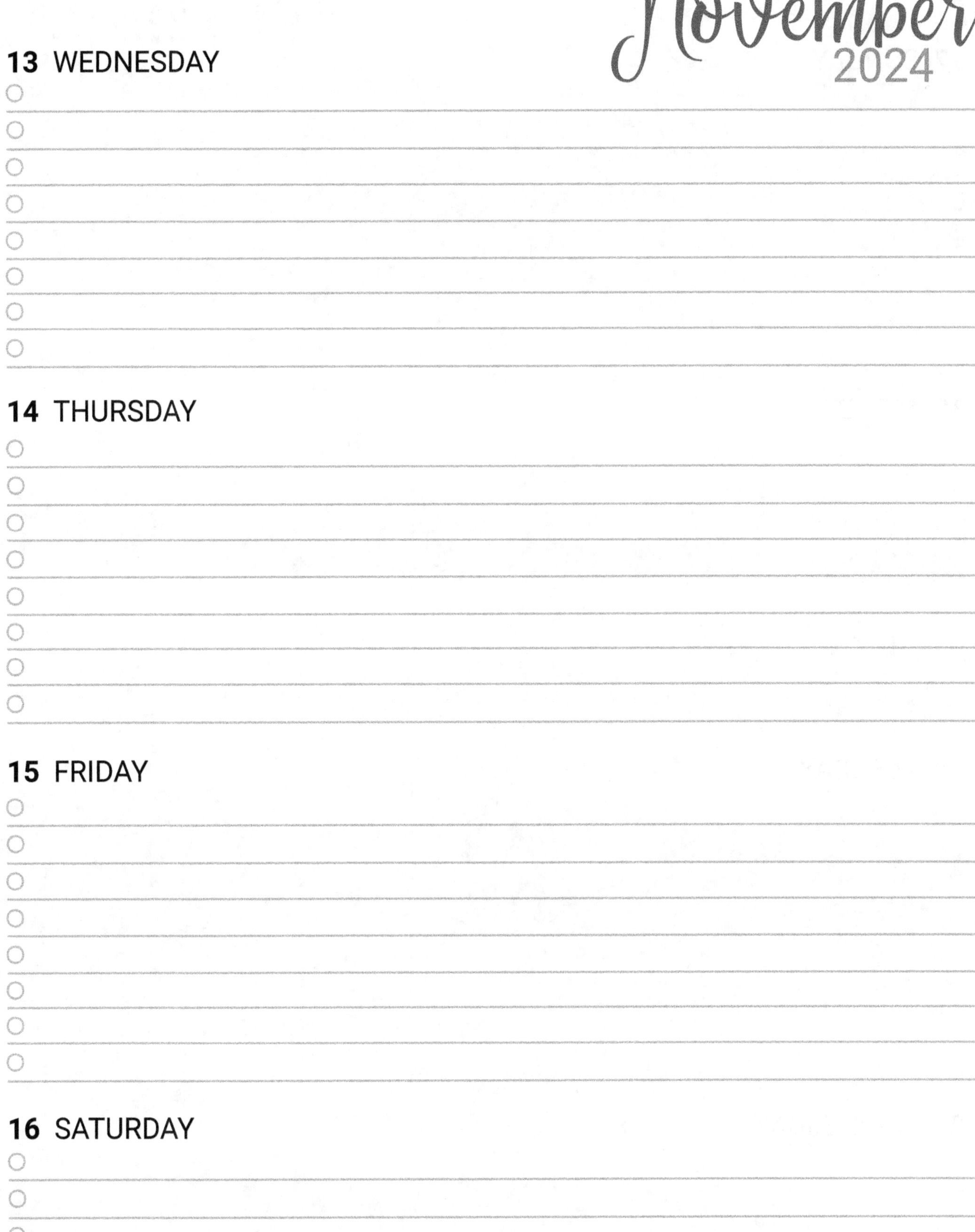

13 WEDNESDAY

14 THURSDAY

15 FRIDAY

16 SATURDAY

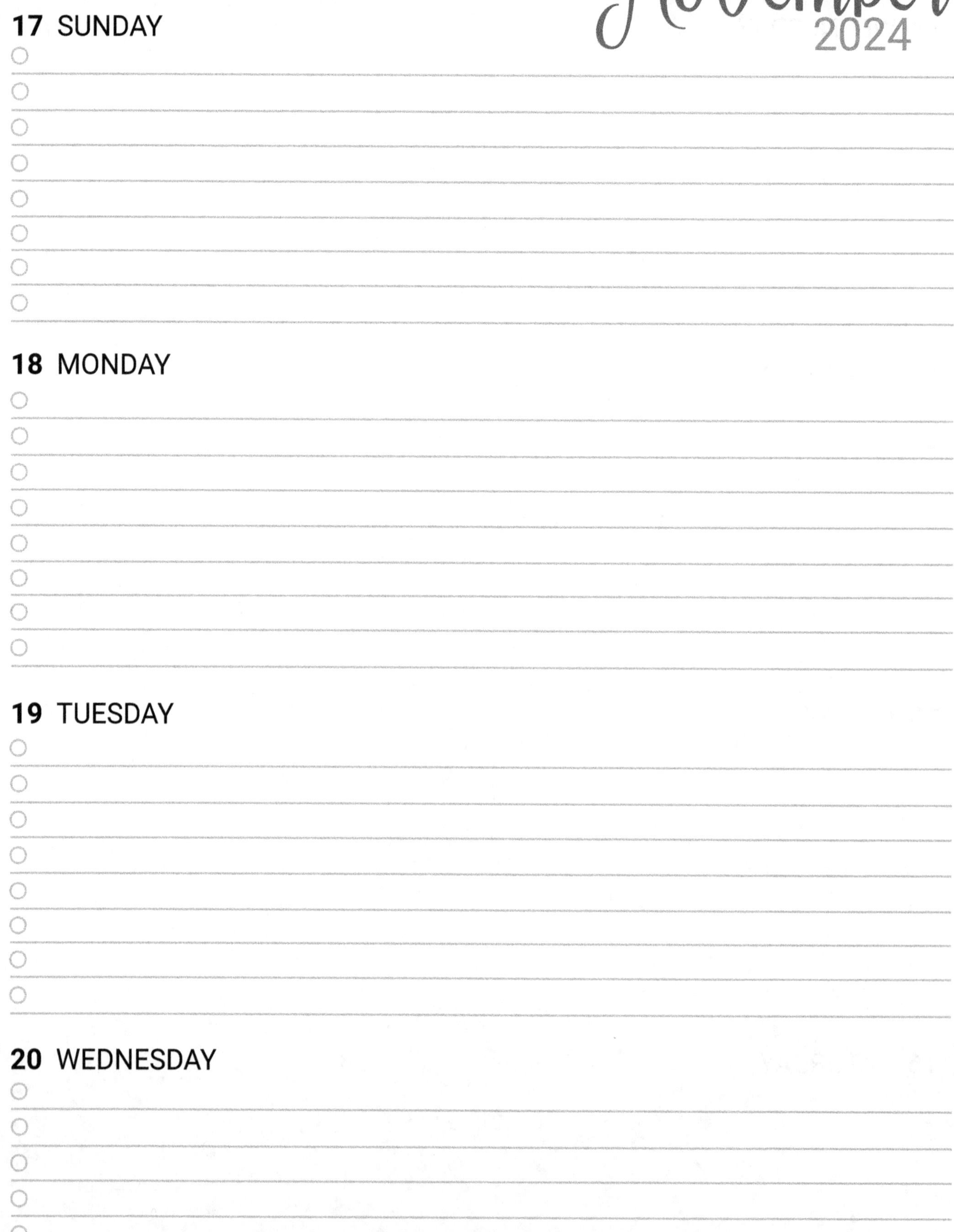

November
2024

17 SUNDAY

18 MONDAY

19 TUESDAY

20 WEDNESDAY

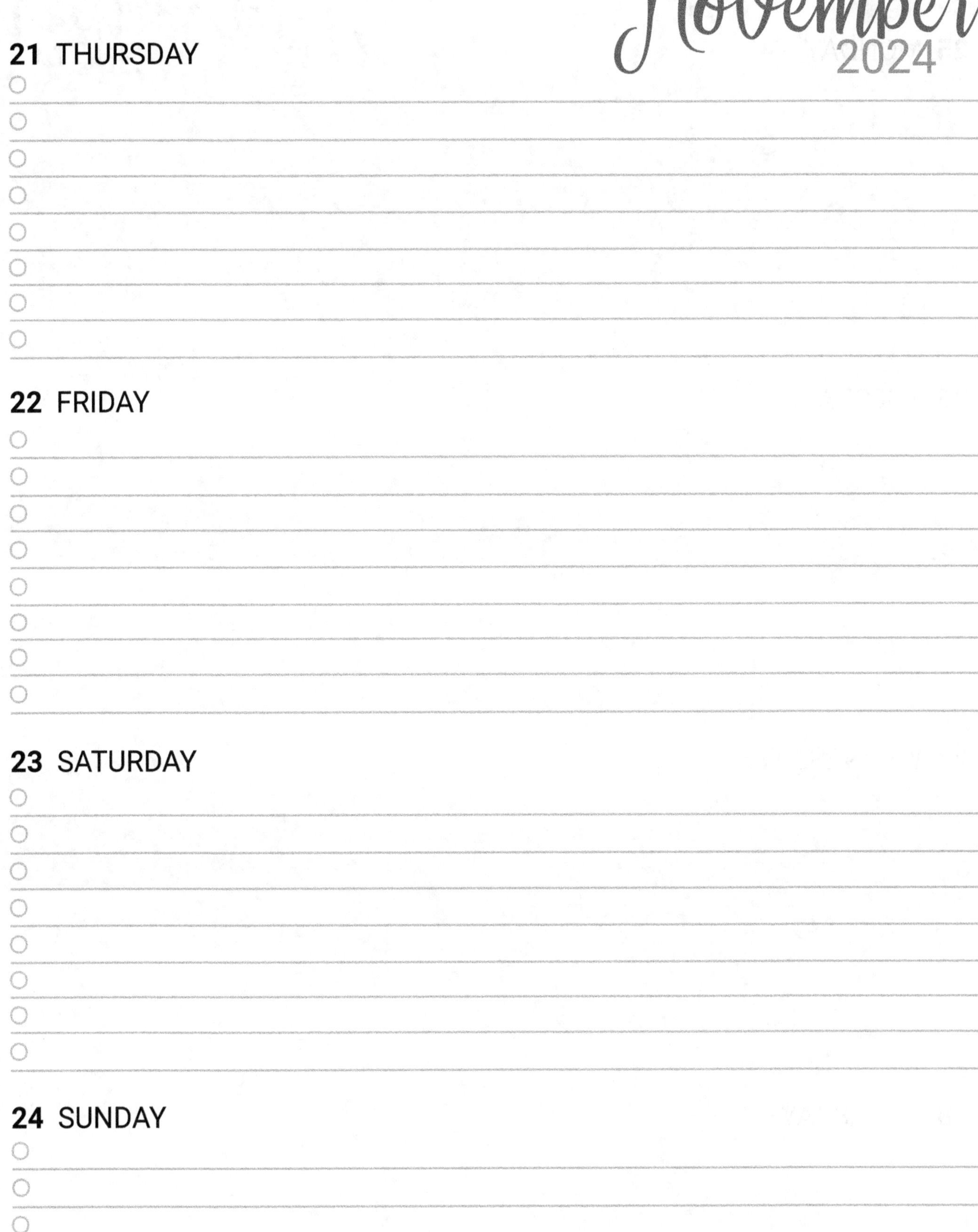

21 THURSDAY

22 FRIDAY

23 SATURDAY

24 SUNDAY

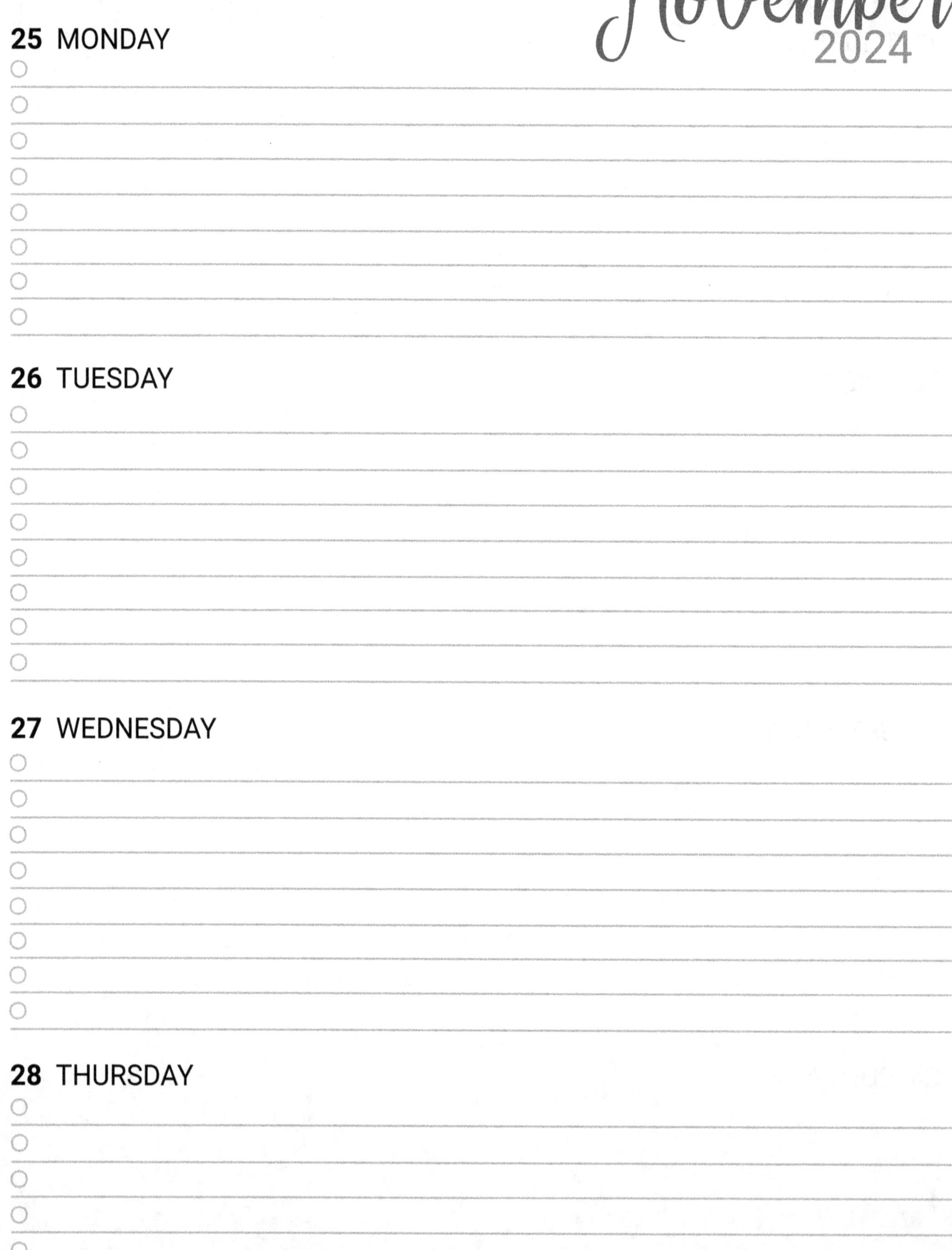

November
2024

25 MONDAY

26 TUESDAY

27 WEDNESDAY

28 THURSDAY

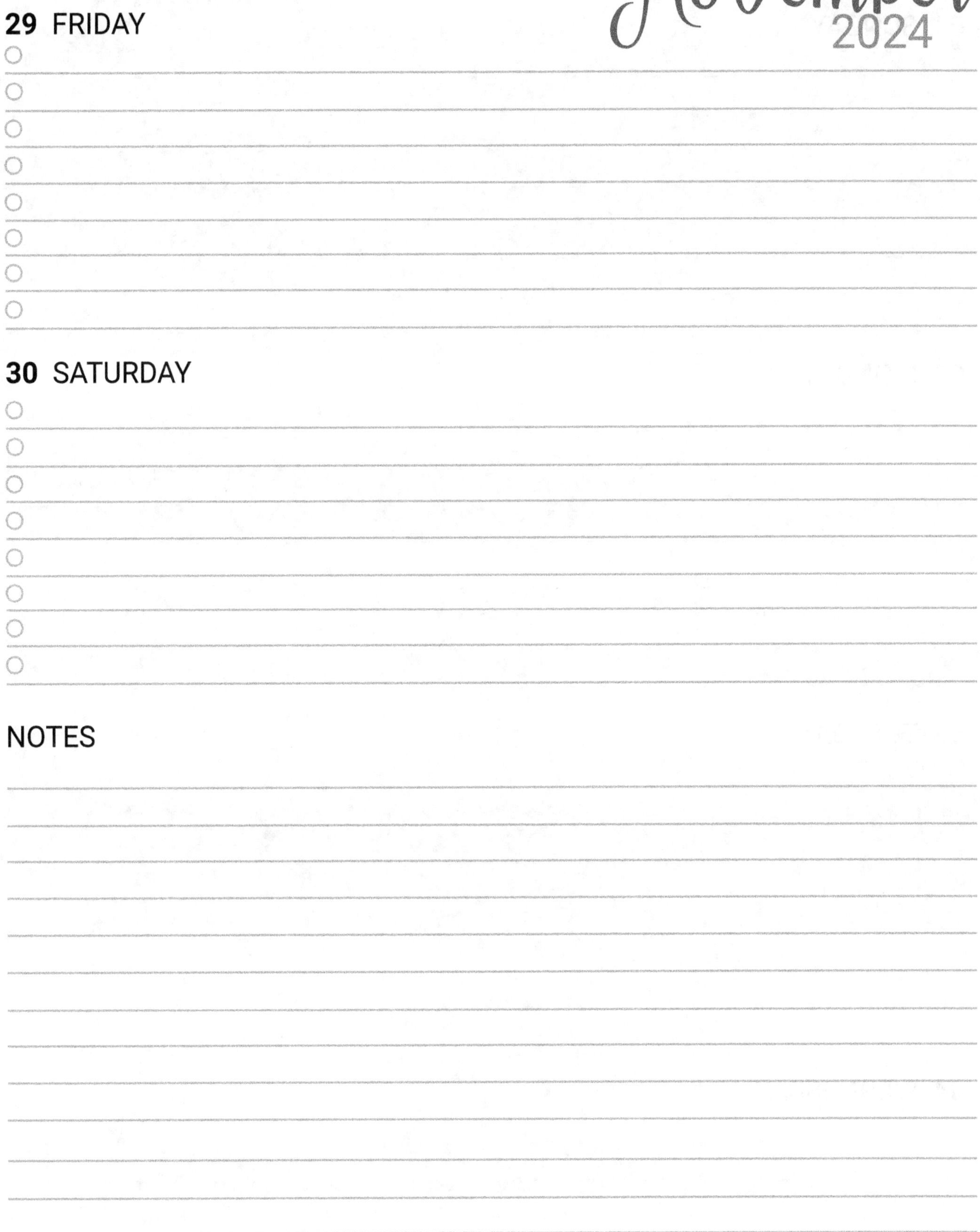

29 FRIDAY

30 SATURDAY

NOTES

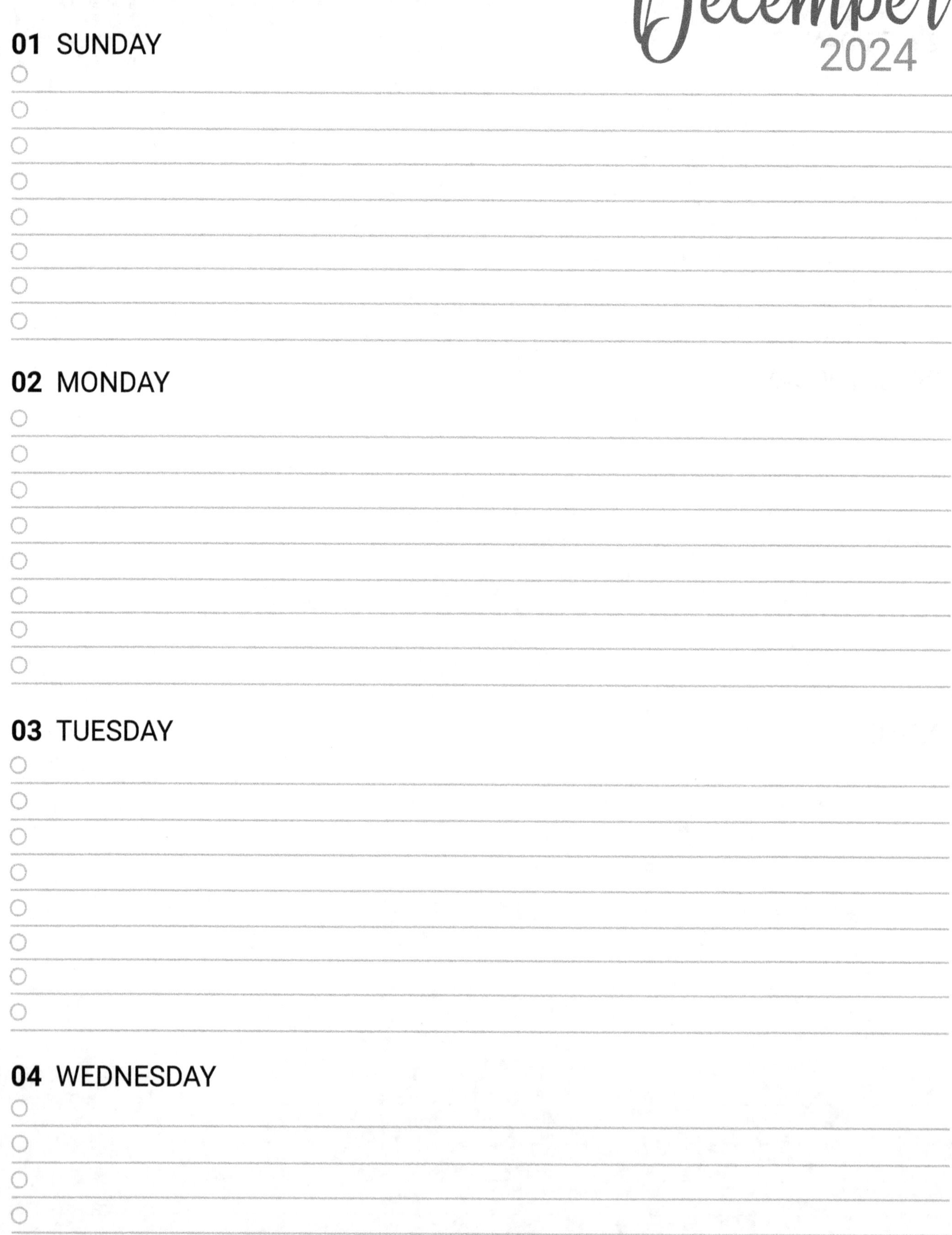

December
2024

01 SUNDAY

02 MONDAY

03 TUESDAY

04 WEDNESDAY

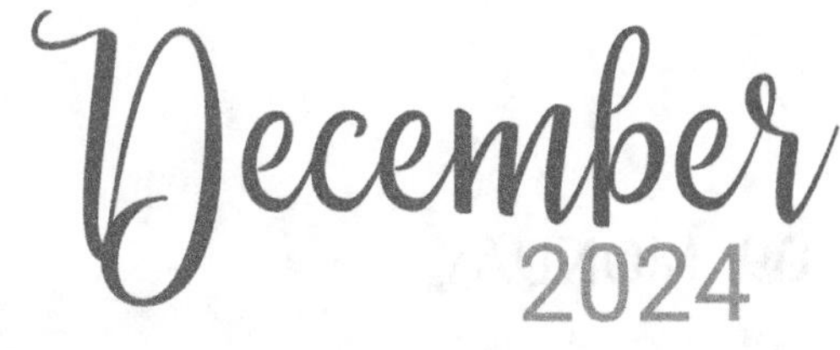

05 THURSDAY

06 FRIDAY

07 SATURDAY

08 SUNDAY

December
2024

09 MONDAY

10 TUESDAY

11 WEDNESDAY

12 THURSDAY

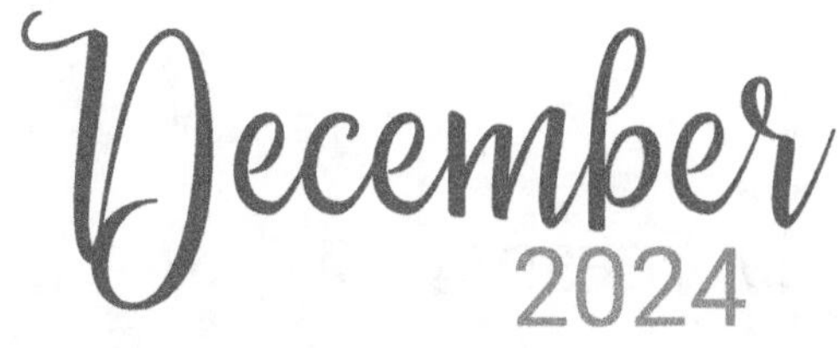

13 FRIDAY

14 SATURDAY

15 SUNDAY

16 MONDAY

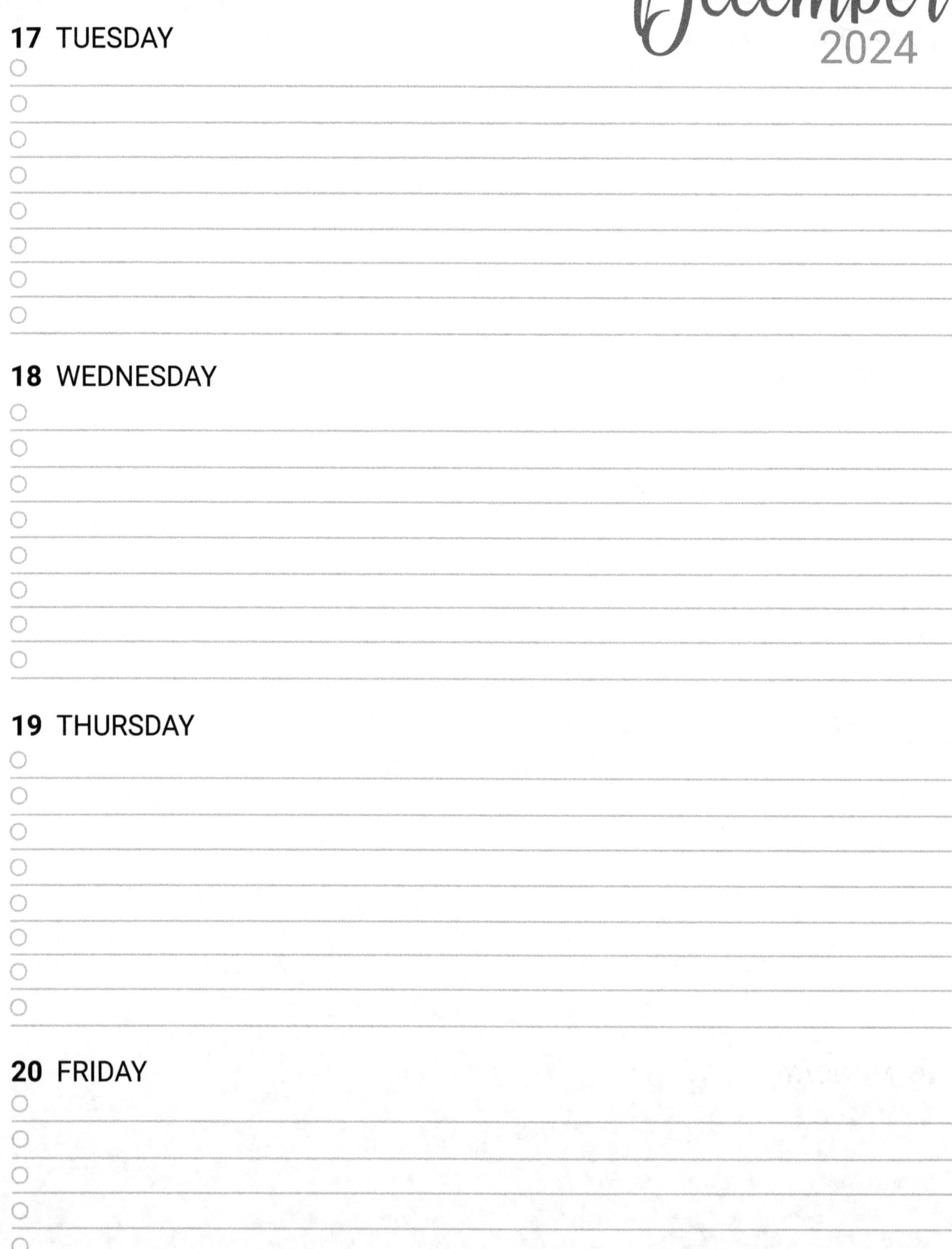

17 TUESDAY

18 WEDNESDAY

19 THURSDAY

20 FRIDAY

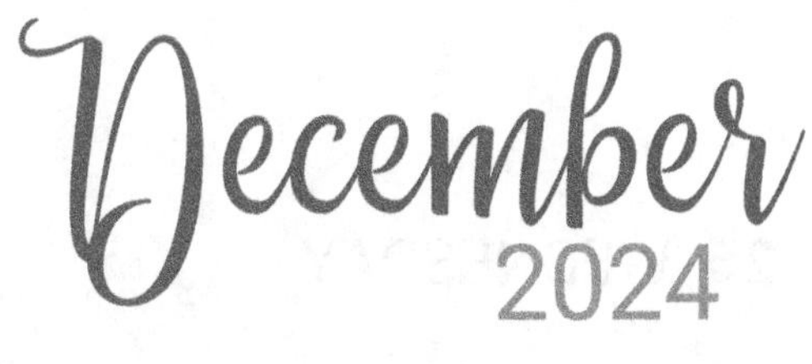

December
2024

21 SATURDAY

22 SUNDAY

23 MONDAY

24 TUESDAY

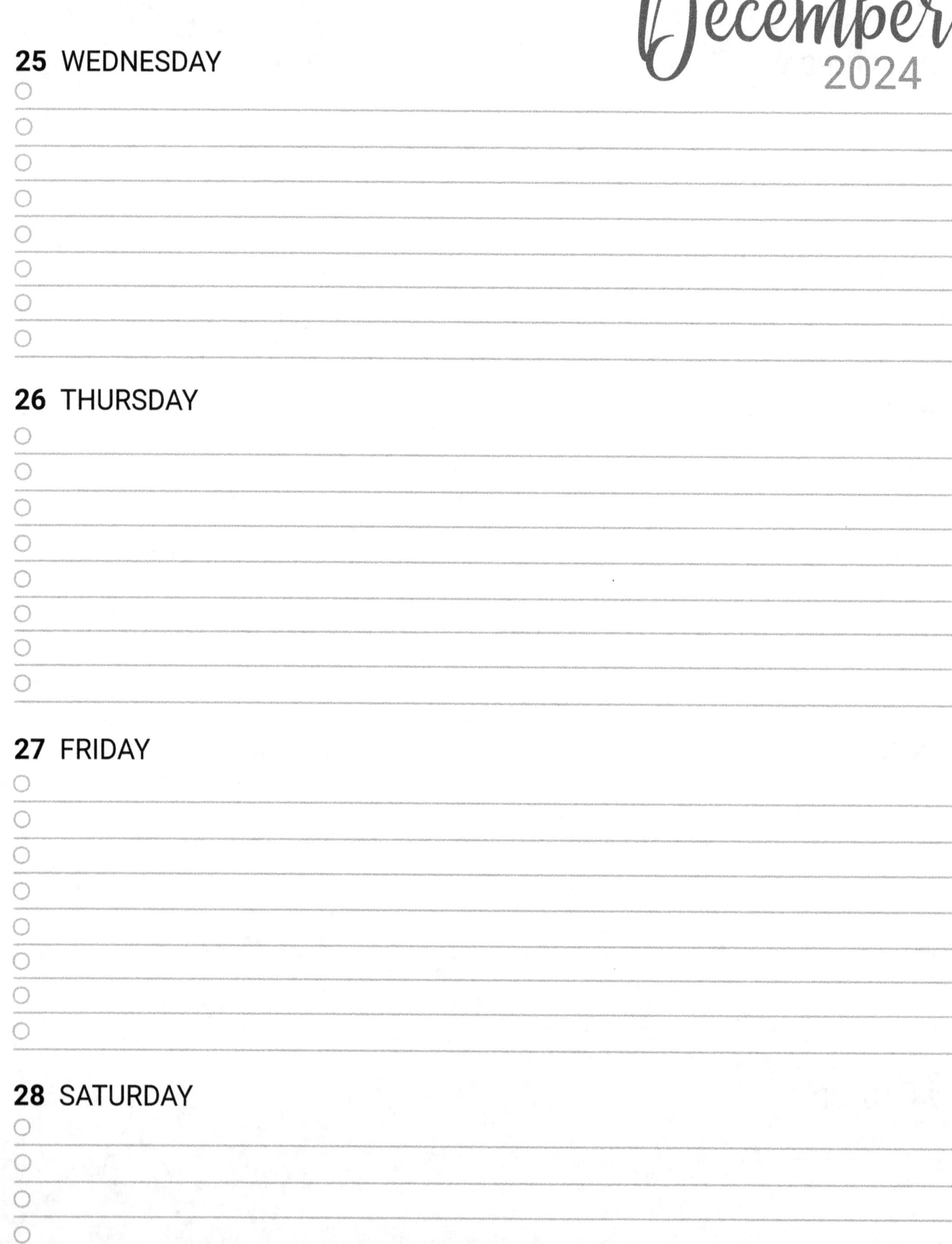

25 WEDNESDAY

26 THURSDAY

27 FRIDAY

28 SATURDAY

29 SUNDAY

30 MONDAY

31 TUESDAY

NOTES

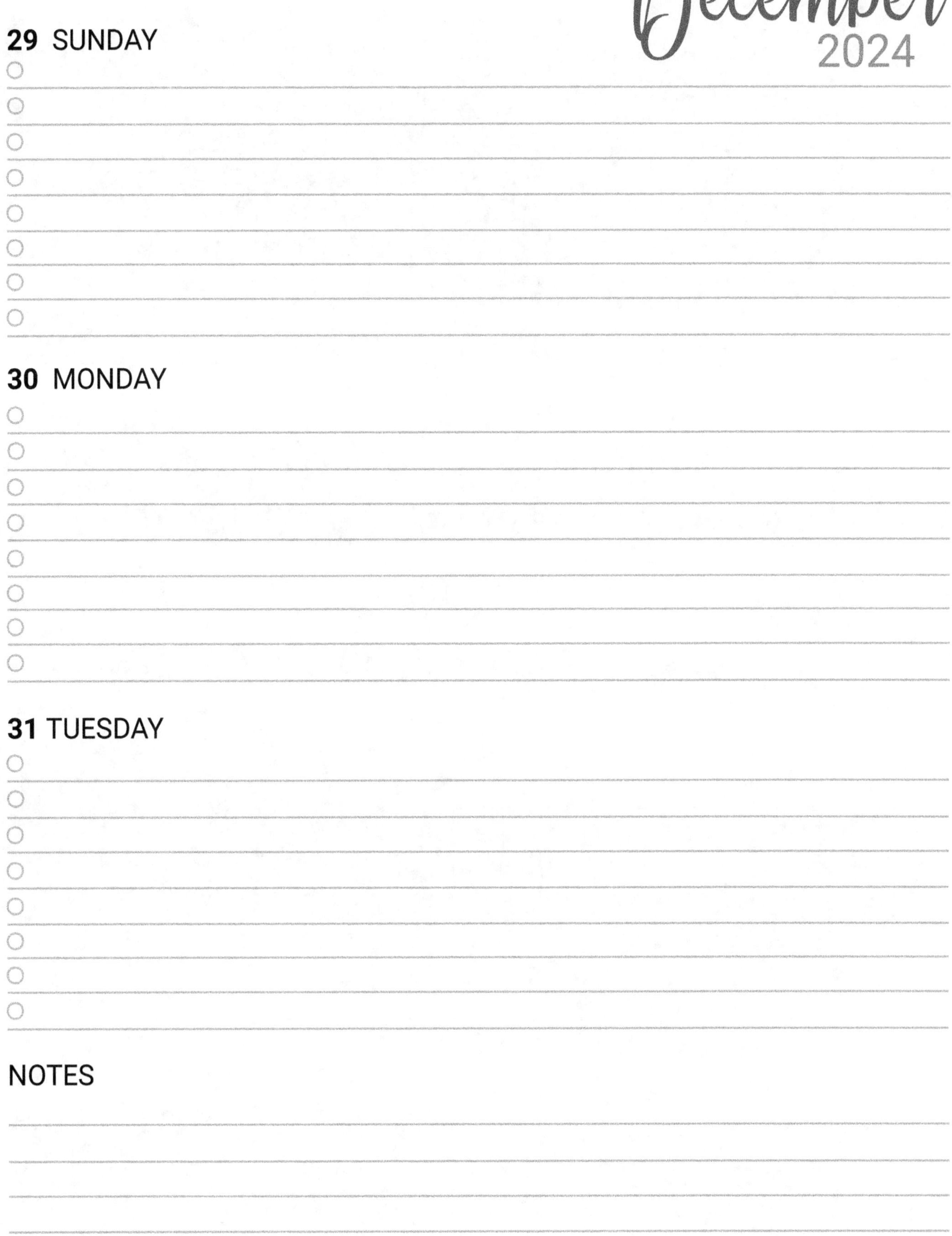

www.ingramcontent.com/pod-product-compliance
Lightning Source LLC
Chambersburg PA
CBHW080343030726
47595CB00013B/4109